Fresh from the Garden

by
Dodi Lee Poulsen
of Two Sisters at
Squirrel Hollow

Landauer Publishing, LLC

Fresh from the Garden

by Dodi Lee Poulsen of Two Sisters at Squirrel Hollow

This book was designed, produced,
and published by Landauer Publishing, LLC
3100 101st Street, Urbandale, IA 50322
www.landauercorp.com   515/287/2144   800/557-2144

President/Publisher: Jeramy Lanigan Landauer
Vice President of Sales and Administration: Kitty Jacobson
Editor: Jeri Simon
Technical Editor: Rhonda Matus
Art Director: Laurel Albright
Photographer: Sue Voegtlin

ISBN 13: 978-1-935726-11-1
ISBN 10:   1-935726-11-0

Library of Congress Control Number: 2011929092
This book printed on acid-free paper.
Printed in United States

10-9-8-7-6-5-4-3-2-1

Dodi Lee Poulsen grew up in Northern California in a close-knit family of two brothers and a sister. Her love of fabric and the art of the needle came honestly and naturally to her. She recalls, *"One of my favorite memories is sitting on my Grandmother's lap when I was about four, helping Nana push fabric through a treadle sewing machine. At ten, with my mother's gentle guidance, I created my first sewn garment, a blouse. It didn't take me long to realize the sewing machine and I would be lifelong partners."*

Dodi's BFA college degree in interior design launched a 25 year career as a free lance interior designer where, in her own company, In the Beginning Creations, she created home decorating projects and devoted many years honing her color and fabric design skills. Quilting has been a passion ever since she created textile projects during college years. For more than 20 years, Dodi has shared her quilting passion, teaching the art of quilting and lecturing to students throughout the country.

In 2006, Dodi and her sister, Heidi began their pattern company, Two Sisters at Squirrel Hollow. Working together in a wonderful quilt studio overlooking the woods on Heidi's 10 acres in Missouri, they have created fresh and youthful patterns that have quickly gained them an enthusiastic following in the quilt market. Dodi's daughter, Megan, has now joined the business as designer for Little Londyn, a children's division of Two Sisters at Squirrel Hollow.

Today, Dodi happily designs and creates quilts at home in the state of Washington as well as during frequent visits to Squirrel Hollow. The beautiful Northwest provides an incredible backdrop for inspiration. Dodi also loves to spend time in her garden where she finds nature creating the best lessons in color and design.

"For me, quilting embraces emotion and beautifully blends fabric with the heart of its creator."

Family life takes center stage for Dodi. She and her husband Bart have raised a son Mikel and a daughter Megan and now have 6 grandchildren. As a new grandmother, she has quickly begun sharing her love of sewing. *"My older grandchildren love to sit on my lap pushing fabric through the sewing machine, just as I did as a child so many years ago."*

Acknowledgements

My love goes out to my family who so often works with my crazy schedule to accommodate me. I am so grateful for your patience, love and endearing support. Each and every one of you make my life an amazing journey.

Table of Contents

Life's a Picnic Collection 16

Table of Contents

Table of Contents

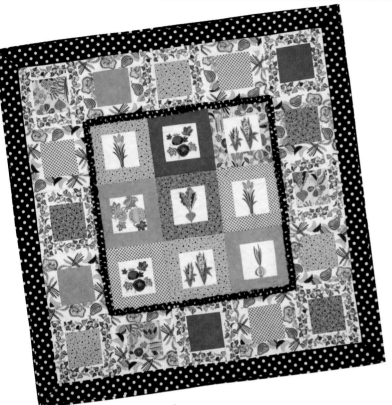

Table of Contents

Fresh from the Garden

As a gardener the product of my labors provide more than just food or beauty for the table. Digging in the dirt can provide clarity and peace to my soul. Dirty fingernails are proof that I have been tending to God's small miracles. Margaret Atwood said, "In the Spring, at the end of the day, you should smell like dirt."

There is nothing I love better than feasting on my favorite vegetables as they come into season each year. Their vibrant colors and delicious freshness are captivating. I can't wait for each season of goodness to come to market.

Larger scale novelty fabrics featuring the abundance of the harvest were my inspiration for the collections in this book. Each year fabric manufacturers duplicate nature at its best on fabrics. Fabrics have never been more beautiful. Big is in… and the bolder the better!

I adore the whimsical nature of novelty fabrics. The projects in this book are equally geared to other fabrics as well. Combine novelty prints with sassy basics and you'll have fabulous projects.

It's amazing what creative energies are released when you step outside your comfort zone. You can create and add your own personal touch using these fun fabrics for yourself and your home, not to mention all the lovely gifts you'll be able to make for friends! Adding that special touch has never been easier.

Included in some of the designs are my favorite pre-cut fabrics. Layer cakes, strips and honey buns can be used in several of the designs that make them simple and easy to create in a short amount of time. Even if you are new to sewing, you can make these delightful projects. Create an entire collection in your favorite fabrics!

I hope you'll enjoy the ideas in my book. Have fun with them and add your own personal style by choosing fabrics and trims reflective of your personal tastes. Here's to Fresh from the Garden goodness!

All My Best,

Dodi

dodipoulsen@twosashquilts.com

www.twosashquilts.com

General Instructions

We do our very best to test & proof our patterns, but sometimes an error will slip by us. Before starting any project we recommend you visit our website at www.twosashquilts.com. We post pattern corrections there. If you catch an error, please let us know. Thank you!

Please read all instructions before beginning any project.

- Yardages are based on 42" fabrics. Please make allowances if your fabric is narrower.

- Seam allowances are 1/4" unless otherwise noted.

- For best results use 100% cotton fabrics from a quality quilt shop. Cotton fabric minimizes seam distortion, presses well and is easy to quilt on.

- Double check all block measurements by laying your clear ruler over the block to ensure correct size. Don't continue to the next step unless they are correct.

- RST means right sides together.

Seam Allowances

We cannot stress enough the importance of accuracy in seam allowances. Test your machine to confirm your seam width. A 1/4"-foot is a life saver and most machines offer this option.

Pressing Tips

- Pressing is the key to successful piecing & quiltmaking. PRESS, do not iron! Don't move the iron back & forth, simply lift the iron up & down & spritz with a little bit of water if necessary. Don't use steam on blocks. Steam can easily distort your fabrics & make them stretch out of shape.

- Most important, every seam must be pressed before the next is added. This will create accuracy & success!

starch

Ever wonder why your quilt blocks don't turn out just right? The correct preparation of the fabric makes all the difference! Starching quilt fabrics makes cutting, piecing, appliquéing and quilting easier. Starched fabric cuts easily, even when stacked together, and sews together beautifully. It will hold sharp creases, including those made by finger pressing. A block made of starched fabric when pressed during construction will not shrink or become otherwise distorted. It's extra work, you say! But It's worth the effort because.....

Starching tames the bias edge. Starch makes all fabrics equal. Homespuns will behave just like batiks, once starched. Starched fabric will give you more control as you stitch. Starched quilt fabric doesn't shift as you rotary cut. Appliqués turn easier with a crisper fold. It makes it easy to make perfect appliquéd circles. Quilting is full of opinions & options. Each quilt is different; each quilter, too. To starch or not to starch is up to you.

My personal favorite starch is a Niagara® non-aerosol spray. Or, you can also easily make your own using 50% water and 50% bottled starch for yardage. STARCH fabrics before starting any project and you won't be disappointed.

Two Sisters Tip

When starching, spray fabric on one side, fold the other half of the fabric on top and press. This way the starch will go directly into the fibers of the fabric and not on your iron. Hooray! It is best to starch more than once - several times does the trick! Reverse the fold and continue starching until you get a crisp piece of fabric.

General Instructions

Pinning

We know you hate to pin, but for the best success, take the time to do it. Pinning reduces slipping, stretching & makes your finished product one you can be proud of.

Nesting seams

When smaller pieced units are required to be pieced together to make a larger block the results will be accurate and polished if you nest the seams. The seams should be pressed in opposite directions from each other so the seam allowance falls in alternate sides of the crossing seam line. Place the 2 units RST matching the seam line. Rub your finger on top and you will see they will nest into each other perfectly. Place a pin on each side of the crossing seam line and stitch into place.

Setting seams

Before you press a seam allowance to one side, put your iron down on it flat, just as it was sewn. Don't move the iron back and forth; just lift the iron up and down. This step "sets" the seam, encouraging the seam to go in the direction of the side on which it was pressed.

No Fuss Fast Fuse Machine Appliqué

Many projects in this book use fusible web and are machine appliquéd to cover the raw edges. It is important to have your machine set up for the best possible results. Following the instructions below, set up your machine in the configuration that will best suit your project.

Machine set-up

1. Make certain your machine is clean and in good working order.
2. Install a new size 60/8, 70/10, 75/11, or 80/12 sharp universal or embroidery needle in your machine.
3. Wind a bobbin with cotton 50 or 60-weight embroidery thread or bobbin-fill thread.
4. Thread the needle with matching or complementary color 50 or 60-weight thread.
5. Set your machine for a zigzag stitch with a width between 1 and 1.5mm or about 1/8" wide. Set the stitch length just above (not at) the satin-stitch setting, or between .5 and 1mm.
6. If possible, set your machine in the "needle down" position and set the motor at half speed.

Machine Appliqué

All pattern pieces are cut without seam allowances. The raw edges are covered with a close machine satin, buttonhole, or decorative stitch.

Using the correct fusible web for your project will be key in its success. Fusible web has an adhesive surface on both sides of the web allowing you to iron it to both the template shape and then onto the fabric.

Currently there are many fusible products to choose from. If you will be hand tracing your deign to the fusible web Lite Steam a Seam 2® or Shades SoftFuse® are ideal.

If you want this to be a painless process try the new Print N' Fuse® fusible webbing. This allows you to print your templates directly onto your webbing without having to trace, saving you an entire step and providing accurate templates! Using this method makes for a NO FUSS FAST FUSE project. Follow manufacturer's instructions for this product.

General Instructions for Fusible Web

First, starch your fabric two or three times following the method stated in the Starch section. This provides a crisp piece that has stability while you cut your shapes out.

Trace or print your template onto the paper side of the fusible web. Leave enough room between shapes to loosely cut them out around the printed or traced line. Do not cut on the traced or printed line at this point. If the shape is more than 2" in diameter it is a good idea to cut out the center of the shape leaving an outer ring of approximately 1/4" – 1/2". This allows the fabric to remain soft and pliable making it easier to quilt and embroider.

Iron the selected fusible web pieces, paper side up, onto the wrong side of fabrics following manufacturer's instructions. Let cool. Cut pieces out directly on the traced or printed line.

Paper Side of Fusible Web

Trace

Wrong Side of Fabric

Position and Fuse

Wrong Side of Fabric

Cut

Arrange pieces onto your quilt block, placing background pieces first, and then work forward layering them.

Peel paper off. Following manufacturer's instructions, fuse appliqué to background fabric.

Right Side of Fabrics

Peel

Arrange and Fuse

Use a stabilizer, tissue paper or a commercially made fabric on the back side while appliquéing. Tear off stabilizer after complete. Using a stabilizer will allow your fabric to move smoothly through the machine when appliquéing while providing stability for the fabric.

Two Sisters Tip

I like to use an appliqué pressing sheet. You can lay out and position your appliqué pieces and fuse them together before you fuse them to your project.

Invisible Applique

Use an invisible thread on the top of your machine & a standard weight thread in the bobbin. This gives the look of hand appliqué in very little time.

Use an invisible blind hem stitch to attach pattern pieces to background fabric. You may need to adjust the tension on your machine.

Bias strips & Binding

Strips for bias binding are cut on the bias, diagonally across the grain of fabric, which runs at a 45-degree angle against the selvage. When the fabric is cut on the bias it allows for the most stretch.

To cut fabric on the bias start with a square or rectangle piece of fabric. Make a cut at a 45-degree angle in the center of the fabric. Cut additional strips out from the center to outer edges utilizing the longer pieces of fabric. (See diagram) Cut strips the desired width parallel to the edge. Cut enough strips to complete the project. The strips will be joined together in the same way as in straight binding.

Bias Binding for Quilt Top

If cutting bias binding for a scalloped or curved edge of a quilt the binding will be a single fold 1" finished piece. Cut the bias strip 1-1/2" wide. Using a 1" bias tape maker, follow manufacturer's instructions to make the tape. Open bias tape on one edge and sew to quilt top. Fold over and hand sew to back side.

Needle sizes

Not all needle sizes are created equal. Stitch quality is affected by the needle and the thread. They go hand in hand and create a successful sewing experience that eliminates skipped stitches, puckered seams, and broken threads. Always start with a fresh, new needle for every sewing project. If stitching problems occur, always change the needle. A dull or burred needle can cause snags and puckering. Select the size of the sewing needle based on the weight of the fabric and the size or type of thread being used.

For general purposes these needles are recommended:

- General Piecing - needle size 80/12
- For machine appliqué – needle size 70/10
- For heavier thread, usually topstitch- needle size 90/14 jeans needle.

It is recommended that you don't use heavy weight thread in your bobbin. You may need to adjust the tension on your machine. When using a heavier weight thread, changing the size of your needle accommodates the thread weight to prevent fraying.

Gathering

Several projects in this book are required to be finished and gathered. Using our favorite tools you will make quick work of what can be tedious.

Two Sisters Tip

Got to have Tools!
A rolled hemming foot is a wonderful sewing machine foot for any project requiring a neat finished edge. It will automatically turn under your hemline or edge 1/4" with just one run through the machine. This foot paired with a gathering foot for your machine will save you time and frustration when making yards of ruffles. When making decorative projects for home or clothing, these are must have sewing feet!

If a gathering foot is unavailable, use dental floss & zigzag over the top, making sure not to catch the floss. This is a great way to gather effectively without using the specialized feet.

To gather, lengthen your stitch to its longest setting. Sew one line close to the top edge of your fabric leaving 4-5 inches of thread on either edge for pulling to gather fabric. Pull the BOBBIN thread gently to gather to the desired length.

Surefire Matching Technique

When you are joining one unit to another it is helpful to use a positioning pin. With RST, push a pin vertically through the intersection of the seam at the 1/4" seam line. Continue pushing pin through bottom block, lining up the 1/4" seam lines.

Keep this pin standing upright so the fabrics won't shift. To hold the fabrics together as shown, pin on either side of the positioning pin, remove the positioning pin. As you sew, remove each pin as it nears the needle.

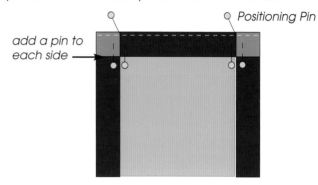

Positioning Pin

add a pin to each side →

Borders

- Measure width of quilt top through center, top & bottom. Take an average of this measurement. Cut the two border pieces to this measurement.

- Sew the two borders to the top & bottom of quilt. Repeat this process for the length of quilt. Press seams toward border.

Using Lengthwise of Fabric for Borders

I like to cut borders from the length of the fabric. This eliminates any seams in the border & makes for a nice flat finish with no "waves". Borders can be a beast to manage when they are wavy. If you cut your borders on the length of the grain, or parallel to the selvage edge, you will eliminate most of the problems. You can use the leftover fabric in the backing or put it in your stash.

Mitered Borders

Mitered borders are not cut to the exact measurement. You will miter them and then cut off the remaining fabric at the end of the process.

1. To find center of border fold it in half and mark with a pin. Place border strip and quilt top RST and sew beginning and ending 1/4" from quilt top corners. Allow excess border fabric to extend beyond edges of quilt top. Repeat for remaining border strips. Back-stitch to secure. Press seams toward border.

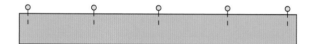

2. Lay quilt top right side up on ironing board or hard surface. Fold each border end flat back onto itself, right sides together, forming a 45-degree angle at the quilt's corner. Press to form sharp creases.

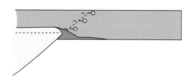

3. Fold quilt on diagonal, right sides together. Align the border strip's raw edges, the border seams at the 1/4" point, and the creases; pin in place. Stitch along crease, backstitching at 1/4" border seam.

4. With quilt right side up, align 45-degree angle line of square ruler on seam line to check accuracy. If corner is flat and square, trim excess fabric to 1/4" seam allowance. Press seam open.

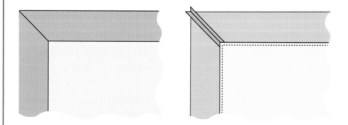

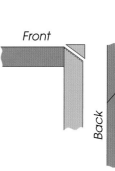

Two Sisters Tip
Border & Block Assembly Pressing Tip
Our favorite tip!

Marrying the border & quilt top is so important for a sharp finished look. It's best to use a flat pressing surface or ironing board when pinning the borders to the quilt. First, find the centers on the quilt & border edges. Place border on the quilt top & PIN to fit within the space. To make sewing easier, use a small burst of steam. The steam will shrink & stretch the fabrics, helping to sandwich the border & quilt top together. Sew & press seam toward border. Do this for all four borders. You will be amazed by the results!

This tip can be used for block assembly too!

Backing

Cut your quilt backing 3" to 5" larger than the quilt top. For large quilts you'll usually have to piece the backing either lengthwise or crosswise. Press the backing fabric before measuring. Always cut the selvages off before sewing the seams together. Use a 1/2" seam allowance and press seams open.

Assembling the Layers

Spread backing, wrong side up, on a flat surface. Anchor it with masking tape or pins being careful not to stretch the backing along the raw edges.

Spread the batting over the backing, smoothing out the wrinkles and lumps.

Place the pressed quilt top over the batting right side up. Make sure the edges are parallel with the edges of the backing fabric to avoid ending up off grain.

Baste the three layers together. Starting in the center each time, baste diagonally to each corner. Continue basting horizontally and vertically until there's enough basting to hold the layers together. You can also use safety pins about 6" to 8" apart instead of basting.

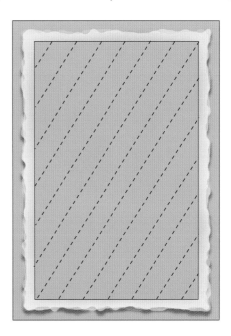

Quilting

All of the quilts shown in this book were machine quilted. Cut batting & backing at least 3" larger than quilt top on all sides. Your quilter will most likely require this.

After quilting, use a rotary cutter to trim backing & batting even with quilt top.

Binding

- Place end of two strips perpendicular to each other forming an 'L', RST. Stitch diagonally & trim to 1/4". Press seam open. Trim the little triangle points that stick out.

- Press in half, wrong sides together to form a long strip. It is important that the corners of the quilt be square at 90-degrees.

- Using a 1/4" seam, attach binding using your favorite technique. Hand or machine sew the binding to the reverse side.

If binding a curved edge see instructions for making bias binding on page 11.

Fresh from the Garden Collections

Life's a Picnic Collection

Give Peas a Chance Collection

Green Thumb Collection

Punkin Collection

Life's a Picnic Quilt

Remember those family outings when mom would spread out a large quilt for
you to sit on with your siblings and you shared her labors of the kitchen?
Afterwards you'd roll on your back with full stomachs and stare at the blue sky with its billowy
clouds, making animals out of their shapes. Who doesn't love a family picnic? Wrap your
family in this blanket of love and make time to enjoy the blessing of just being together.

Finished size: approximately 65-1/2" x 82-1/2"

For use with 10" squares or layer cakes, 2-1/2" strips or jelly rolls and 1-1/2" strips or honey buns. All three sizes are used and make the work a piece of cake.

Fabric Requirements

Fabric A	1-1/2 yards vegetable focal **or** 20 precut 10" x 10" squares for blocks
Fabric B	9 neutral fabrics, 1/2 yard of each **or** 36 precut 1-1/2" strips **and** 36 precut 2-1/2" strips for blocks
Fabric C	3/4 yard orange print for inner border
Fabric D	2-7/8 yards green print for outer border, prairie points, and binding
Fabric E	5 yards backing
Fabric F	Assorted scraps for vegetable appliqués

Lightweight fusible web

Cutting Guide

Fabric A:
- Cut 5 strips 10" x WOF
  Sub cut into 20 squares 10" x 10" for blocks

Fabric B:
- Cut 4 strips 2-1/2" x WOF from each of the 9 fabrics for a total of 36 strips for blocks
- Cut 4 strips 1-1/2" x WOF from each of the 9 fabrics for a total of 36 strips for blocks

From Fabric C:
- Cut 7 strips 2-1/2" x WOF for inner border

Fabric D:
- Cut 7 strips 5-1/2" x WOF for outer border
- Cut 4 strips 2-3/4" x WOF
  Sub cut into 56 squares 2-3/4" x 2-3/4" for prairie points
- Cut 8 strips 2-1/4" x WOF for binding

Two Sisters Tip

When sewing long strips of fabric together it is helpful to cut the length into 2 pieces if the project allows. This helps eliminate the "wave" that can often occur when piecing long strips together. For this project cutting the strips in half will be very helpful.

Pieced Strip Squares

1. Cut the 36 Fabric B 2-1/2"-wide strips and the 36 Fabric B 1-1/2"-wide strips in half to make 144 half-strips that are approximately 21" long.

2. Select 4, 1-1/2"-wide half-strips and 3, 2-1/2"-wide half-strips. With right sides facing, use a 1/4" seam allowance to sew these together in any order along the long edges. Press the seams in one direction. The pieced strip fabric rectangle should measure approximately 21" x 10-1/2".

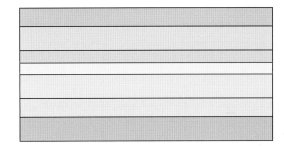

3. Continue sewing the half-strips together to make a total of 14 pieced rectangles, each measuring no less than 10" x approximately 21". Be creative, mixing up the fabric and strip sizes in any combination; there will be leftover half-strips.

4. From 4 of the pieced rectangles, cut 8, 9" x 9" square blocks for the center section; set these aside. Cut the 10 remaining rectangles in half to make 20 pieced strip squares for the half-square triangles.

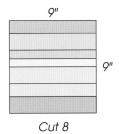

9"

9"

Cut 8

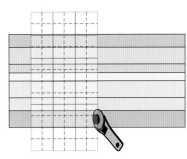

Cut to make 20

Half-square Triangles

1. Draw a diagonal line from corner to corner on the wrong side of the Fabric A 10" x 10" squares.

2. Place a Fabric A 10" x 10" square on a pieced strip square, RST, positioning it so it is horizontally in line with the strips. Sew 1/4" on either side of the drawn line. Cut on the drawn line to make 2 half-square triangles. Press seam toward Fabric A and trim to 9" x 9".

3. Repeat Step 2 to make 40 half-square triangles.

Pinwheel Blocks

1. Sew the half-square triangles together in pairs as shown. Press seams open.

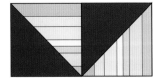

2. Join 2 pairs to form a block. Press seams open. Make 10 blocks. Blocks will measure 17-1/2" x 17-1/2".

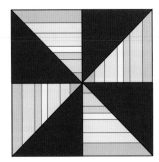

Make 10

Two Sisters Tip

Chain piecing

The fastest way to piece a large number of blocks is to put them together at the same time without stopping to cut threads. Place the first two pieces of fabric to be joined under the presser foot and sew from edge to edge. Feed the next two pieces without cutting your thread until all pieces have been joined. Cut threads to separate.

Nesting seams

Nesting seams will enable the seams to match perfectly. Nesting is possible when the seams are pressed in opposite directions. For the pinwheel, when seams are laid on top of each other, RST, they will fit snugly against each other. Rub your finger over the seams and they will slide into place; pin.

Center section

1. Lay out 8, 9" x 9" pieced strip squares in 4 rows of 2, alternating the direction of the strips in a checkerboard pattern.

2. Sew together one row at a time. Press seams in opposite directions for each row. Sew rows together to make the center section.

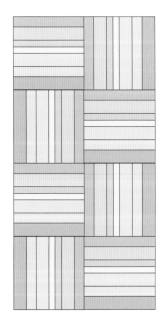

3. Trace tomato templates on page 21 onto fusible web. Cut the shapes out approximately 1/8" outside the traced lines. Press fusible web shapes, paper side up, onto the wrong side of the Fabric F scraps. Cut out the appliqué shapes on the drawn lines.

4. Position the appliqué shapes on the center section, referring to the photograph on page 21 for placement. Fuse in place.

5. Appliqué the shapes using your method of choice. Matching thread was used to buttonhole-stitch over the raw edges of each shape.

Prairie Points

1. Fold each Fabric D 2-3/4" x 2-3/4" square in half diagonally with wrong sides facing and press.

2. Fold each in half again on the diagonal to make a total of 56 smaller triangles; press. These are the prairie points.

Make 56

3. Pin the prairie points to the right side of the center section, aligning the long raw edge of each prairie point with the raw edge of the center section as shown. Overlap the points slightly by slipping the folded edge of a prairie point into the open side of the adjacent triangle. Adjust the overlap as needed to fit 9 points along the short edges of the center section and 19 on the long edges. Baste the points onto the center section.

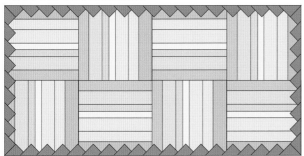

Assembly

1. Sew 3 pinwheel blocks together to make the top row. Press seams toward the center block. Repeat for the bottom row.

Make 2

2. Sew the 4 remaining pinwheel blocks together in pairs. Sew these to either side of the center section. Press seams toward the pinwheel blocks.

3. Sew the top and bottom rows to the remaining edges of the center section to complete the quilt center. Press seams away from the center section.

19

Borders

1. Piece the Fabric C 2-1/2" x WOF inner border strips to make the following: 2, 2-1/2" x 68-1/2" for sides and 2, 2-1/2" x 65-1/2" for top and bottom. From the leftover strips, cut 4, 2-1/2" x 5-1/2" strips.

2. Piece the Fabric D 5-1/2" x WOF outer border strips to make the following: 2, 5-1/2" x 68-1/2" for sides and 2, 5-1/2" x 51-1/2" for top and bottom. From the leftover strips, cut 4, 5-1/2" x 5-1/2" squares.

3. Sew together the side inner and outer border strips. Press seams toward outer border. Sew these to the sides of the quilt center. Press seams toward border.

4. Sew Fabric C 2-1/2" x 65-1/2" inner border strips to the top and bottom edges of the quilt center. Press seams toward the border.

5. Join Fabric D 5-1/2" x 51-1/2" top outer border strips, Fabric D 5-1/2" x 5-1/2" squares, and Fabric C 2-1/2" x 5-1/2" strips to make pieced outer border strips. Press seams away from center.

Make 2

6. Sew the pieced outer border strips to the top and bottom edges of the quilt center. Press seams toward outer borders.

Finishing

1. Refer to General Instructions – Backing and Assembling the Layers on page 13.

2. Quilt as desired.

3. Refer to General Instructions – Binding on page 13 to bind the quilt using the Fabric D 2-1/4" x WOF strips.

All templates are reversed

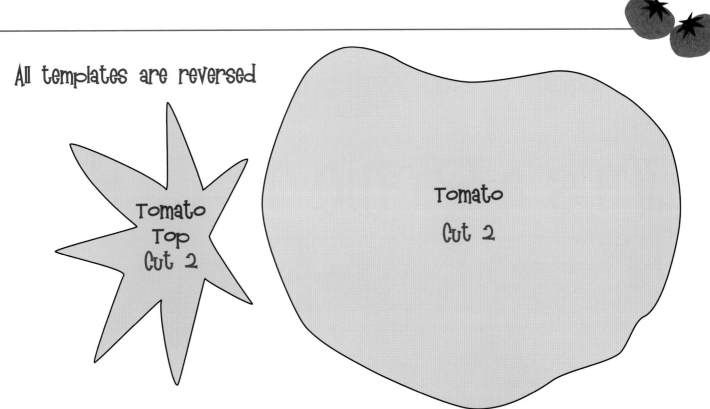

Tomato
Top
Cut 2

Tomato
Cut 2

Life's a Picnic Quilt

Life's a Picnic Tote Bag

Finished size: approximately 20-1/4" x 12" x 4"

Fabric Requirements

Fabric A	1/2 yard vegetable focal for front and back
Fabric B	1-1/4 yards flower print for sides, handle, small front pocket, and inside pockets
Fabric C	3/8 yard green for large front pocket
Fabric D	7/8 yard orange for lining
Fabric E	1/8 yard green print for bag binding
Fabric F	1/4 yard red for pocket binding and lining

8-1/2" x 11" sheet of printable fabric

Lightweight batting

Lightweight fusible web

Lightweight fusible batting

2 large snaps

6-1/2" x 20-1/2" plastic rectangle for bottom

Cutting Guide

Fabric A:
- Cut 2 rectangles 22" x 15" for bag front and back

Fabric B:
- Cut 2 strips 4" x WOF for straps
- Cut 1 rectangle 21" x 19" for inside pocket
- Cut 1 rectangle 21" x 14" for inside pocket
- Cut 2 rectangles 8" x 15" for sides
- Cut 1 rectangle 8" x 22" for bottom
- Cut 1 rectangle 9-1/2" x 7-1/4" for small front pocket

Fabric C:
- Cut 1 rectangle 12" x 18-1/2" for large front pocket

Fabric D:
- Cut 2 rectangles 21" x 14" for front and back lining
- Cut 2 rectangles 7" x 14" for side lining
- Cut 1 rectangle 7" x 21" for bottom lining

Fabric E:
- Cut 2 strips 1-3/4" x WOF for bag binding

Fabric F:
- Cut 1 strip 1-1/2" x 16" for pocket binding
- Cut 1 rectangle 9-1/2" x 7-1/4" for small pocket lining

Batting:
- Cut 2 rectangles 17" x 24" for front and back
- Cut 2 rectangles 10" x 17" for sides
- Cut 1 rectangle 10" x 24" for bottom
- Cut 1 rectangle 12" x 9-1/4" for large front pocket
- Cut 2 strips 1-3/4" x 42" for straps

Fusible Batting:
- Cut 2 rectangles 21" x 14" for front and back lining
- Cut 2 rectangles 7" x 14" for side lining
- Cut 1 rectangle 7" x 21" for bottom lining

Two Sisters Tip

To make the fabric for the tote a bit sturdier it is easy to quilt the fabric on the sewing machine before assembly.

Prepare Focal Fabric

1. Use chalk or water-soluble marker to draw lines on the Fabric A 22" x 15" front and back rectangles. Space the lines 1-1/2" apart and at a 30-degree angle across the rectangles.

2. Center a Fabric A rectangle right side up on a 17" x 24" batting rectangle; approximately 1" of batting will extend beyond the edges of the fabric. Smooth out the fabric and pin or spray baste in place on the batting. Sew on the drawn lines. Repeat for the second Fabric A rectangle.

3. Repeat Steps 1 and 2 for the Fabric B 8" x 15" side rectangles and Fabric B 8" x 22" bottom rectangle, only draw lines vertically across the fabric.

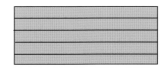

4. Trim the quilted fabric for the front and back to measure 14" x 21". Trim the sides to measure 7" x 14" and the bottom to measure 7" x 21".

Front Pockets

1. Use your computer to type "Life's a Picnic!" in two lines in the font of your choice. Adjust the font size as needed so the saying measures approximately 5" x 3". Print the saying in brown ink on the printable fabric. **Note:** Scrap Swirl font size 175 was used for this project or you can copy the image on page 25.

2. Press an 8" x 6" rectangle of fusible web, paper side up, onto the wrong side of the printable fabric behind the saying. Use a pinked rotary cutter or pinking shears to trim the printable fabric into a 6-3/4" x 4" rectangle with the saying centered.

3. Center the "Life's a Picnic!" rectangle on Fabric B 9-1/2" x 7-1/4" small front pocket; fuse in place. Stitch 1/4" inside the pinked edge of the printed rectangle to secure.

4. Sew Fabric F 9-1/2" x 7-1/4" small pocket lining to Fabric B small pocket RST, leaving a 4" opening in the bottom edge. Turn right side out and press.

5. Fold Fabric C 12" x 18-1/2" large front pocket in half to measure 12" x 9-1/4"; press. Center the small pocket on one half of the large pocket with the top of the small pocket toward the large pocket's center fold. Sew the small pocket to the large pocket along the side and bottom edges.

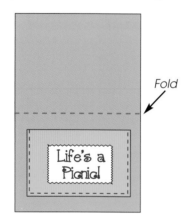

Fold

6. Fold the large pocket in half with the 12" x 9-1/4" batting rectangle between the layers. Baste the side edges together. Refer to General Instructions – Binding on page 13 to bind the top edge of the large pocket with the Fabric F 1-1/2" x 16" pocket binding strip, using a decorative stitch if desired.

Binding

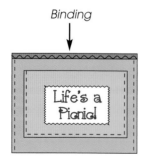

7. Center the pocket on the quilted bag front, aligning the bottom edges. Baste along the side and bottom edges.

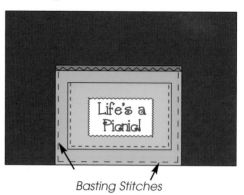

Basting Stitches

straps

1. Press under 1/4" on both long edges of a Fabric B 4" x WOF strap. Fold the strap in half lengthwise with the 1-3/4" x 42" batting strip between the layers. Repeat for the second strap.

2. Measure 9-1/4" in from the short ends of each strap and mark with a pin or chalk. Sew the side edges of both straps closed between the marks. Sew additional lines of stitching between the marks at the center and folded edges to reinforce the strap handle area.

3. Pin one strap on the bag front, overlapping the side edges of the large pocket by 1/4" and aligning the raw edges at the bottom. Sew strap to the bag front along both long edges, sewing from the bottom of the bag front to the marks on the strap. Reinforce the strap area just below the marks by sewing a large "X".

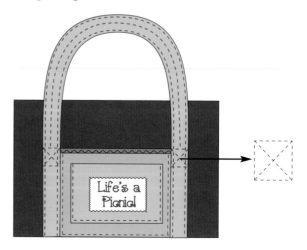

24

4. Attach the remaining strap to the quilted bag back in the same manner, measuring so the placement is the same as on the front.

Assembly of Bag and Lining

1. Sew the quilted side and bottom pieces together, adding a 7" x 14" side to each short edge of the 7" x 21" bottom to make one long strip.

2. Pin one long edge of the side/bottom strip to the bag front RST, easing to fit. Sew, rounding the corners at the bottom of the bag. Sew the opposite edge of the side/bottom strip to the bag back in the same manner. Clip corners. Turn bag right side out.

3. Mark placement of snaps on side panels of bag 2-1/2" from top edge and 1-1/2" from side seams. Add snaps to bag following manufacturer's instructions.

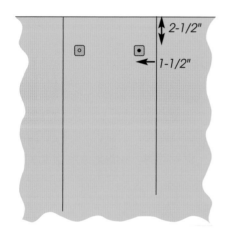

4. Fuse batting to the wrong side of the Fabric D 21" x 14", 7" x 14", and 7" x 21" lining pieces.

5. Fold the Fabric B 21" x 19" and 21" x 14" inside pockets in half to measure 21" x 9-1/2" and 22" x 7". Draw lines as shown to divide each inside pocket into 3 sections.

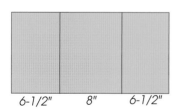
6-1/2"   8"   6-1/2"

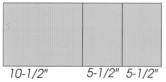
10-1/2"   5-1/2"   5-1/2"

6. Place the inside pockets on the right side of the Fabric D 21" x 14" front and back lining rectangles, aligning the bottom edges. Baste at the side and bottom edges. Sew on the drawn lines of pockets

through all layers, backstitching at the top edge to reinforce.

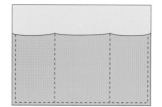 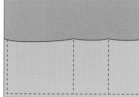

7. Sew the lining pieces together following Steps 1 and 2 for the bag. Do not turn lining.

8. Insert the lining into bag with wrong sides together; baste the top edges together.

9. Sew together the short ends of the Fabric E 1-3/4" x WOF binding strips to make one long strip. Press seam open. Press under 1/4" on one long edge of binding.

10. Working on the lining side of bag, sew the remaining long edge of binding to bag. Trim and join ends of binding to fit. Fold binding over to the outside of bag and sew in place 1" down from top edge. Use a decorative stitch if desired.

11. Place plastic rectangle in the bottom of bag to add stability and support.

12. Attach a plastic embellishment with ribbon to the front pocket if desired.

Life's a Picnic!
Enlarge to 150%

Life's a Picnic Napkin

Makes 1 napkin

Fabric Requirements

Fabric A   22" x 22" square solid fabric for napkin

Fabric B   1-3/4" x 22" strip contrasting
solid fabric for band

Printable fabric

Lightweight fusible web

Assembly

1. Use your computer to type "Life's a picnic!" in the font of your choice. Adjust the font size as needed so the saying measures approximately 2-1/4" long. Print the saying in brown ink on the printable fabric. **Note:** Curlycue font size 37 was used for this project.

2. Press a 2" x 4" rectangle of fusible web, paper side up, onto the wrong side of the printable fabric behind the saying. Trim the printable fabric to 2-1/2" x 3/4" with the saying centered.

3. Press a 1-3/4" x 22" strip of fusible web, paper side up, onto the wrong side of the Fabric B 1-3/4" x 22" band strip. Use a pinked rotary cutter or pinking shears to trim the long edges of the band to measure 1-1/4" x 22".

4. Position "Life's a picnic!" rectangle on the band 5" from the right end; fuse in place. Use a narrow satin stitch over the raw edges of rectangle.

Finished napkin size:
approximately 19" x 19"

5"

5. Position band on the Fabric A 22" x 22" napkin square, 5" from the bottom edge; fuse in place. Sew just inside each pinked edge of the strip to secure.

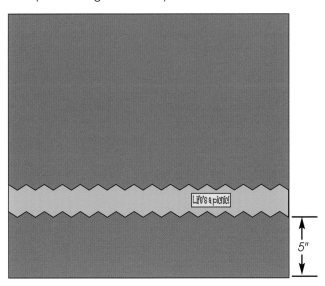

5"

6. Fold napkin in half diagonally RST, aligning the raw edges. Beginning at one corner, make a mark on the raw edge 2-1/2" from the corner and another mark on the folded edge 2" from the corner. Draw a straight line connecting the two marks. Sew on the drawn line, stopping 1/4" from the raw edges. Trim away the corner leaving a 1/4" seam allowance; press the seam open. Turn corner right side out; press well. Repeat for each corner.

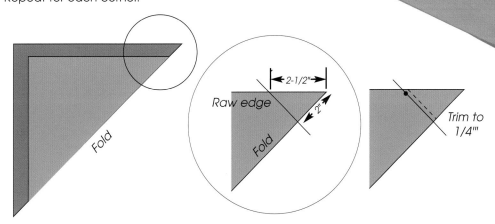

Fold

Raw edge

2-1/2"

2"

Fold

Trim to 1/4'"

7. To hem, press under 1/4" along all raw edges, including the short edges of the band in the hem. Sew close to the pressed edges.

Give Peas a Chance Quilt

I love eating fresh peas right out of the pod. Most of the time, my peas never make it into a pot. Adding a touch of whimsy to your table will be a snap with this table quilt and accompanying projects. Giving Peas a Chance never looked this good!

Finished size: approximately 48-1/2" x 51-1/2"

Fabric Requirements

Fabric A   1-3/4 yards pea focal for
half-square triangles and binding

Fabric B   6 polka dot fabrics, 1/2 yard of
each for half-square triangles

Fabric C   3 yards white for border
and backing

Fabric D   10, 6" x 12" rectangles in 10 colors
for flower appliqués

Batting   54" x 57"

Heavyweight fusible web
10, 6" x 6" squares

Cutting Guide

Fabric A:
- Cut 9 strips 5-1/2" x WOF
  Sub cut into 60 squares 5-1/2" x 5-1/2"
- Cut 5 strips 2-1/4" x WOF for binding

Fabric B:
- Cut 2 strips 5-1/2" x WOF
  from each of the 6 fabrics
  Sub cut into 10 squares 5-1/2" x 5-1/2"
  for a total of 60 squares

Fabric C:
- Cut 2 strips 6" x 48-1/2" for border

Half-square Triangles

1. Draw a diagonal line from corner to
   corner on the wrong side of the Fabric A
   5-1/2" x 5-1/2" squares.

2. Place a Fabric A 5-1/2" x 5-1/2" square on
   a Fabric B 5-1/2" x 5-1/2" square, RST and
   aligning the edges. Sew 1/4" on either side of
   the drawn line. Cut on the drawn line to
   make 2 half-square triangles. Press seam to
   the dark fabric and trim to 4-1/2" x 4-1/2".

3. Repeat Step 2 to make 20 half-square
   triangles of each of the Fabric A/B
   combinations for a total of 120
   half-square triangles.

Assembly

1. Sew together 20 same-color half-square triangles to make 2
   rows as shown. Press seams in opposite directions. Join the rows
   to make a zigzag unit. Repeat to make 6 zigzag units, 1 of
   each Fabric A/B color combination.

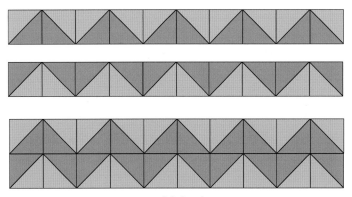

Make 6

2. Sew the zigzag units together to complete the quilt center.
   Press seams in one direction.

29

3. Join the Fabric C 6" x 48-1/2" border strips to the long edges of the quilt center. Press seams toward the border.

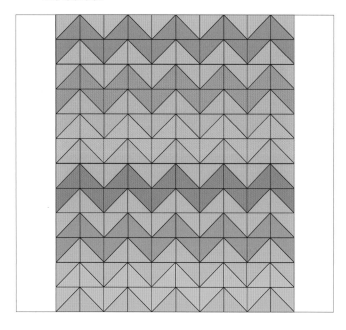

Finishing

1. Refer to General Instructions – Backing and Assembling the Layers on page 13.

2. Quilt as desired.

3. Fold a Fabric D 6" x 12" rectangle in half with wrong sides together to make a 6" x 6" square. To stiffen fabric, insert a 6" x 6" square of heavyweight fusible web between the fabric layers and fuse. Trace the flower template onto one side of stiffened fabric and satin-stitch just inside traced line. Trim away fabric beyond satin stitching. Repeat to make 10 flowers.

4. Position 5 flowers evenly spaced on each Fabric C border referring to the photo on page 31. Quilt in place, sewing from the center of the flower outward as desired, leaving the ends of the petals loose.

5. Refer to General Instructions – Binding on page 13 to bind the quilt using the Fabric A 2-1/4" x WOF strips.

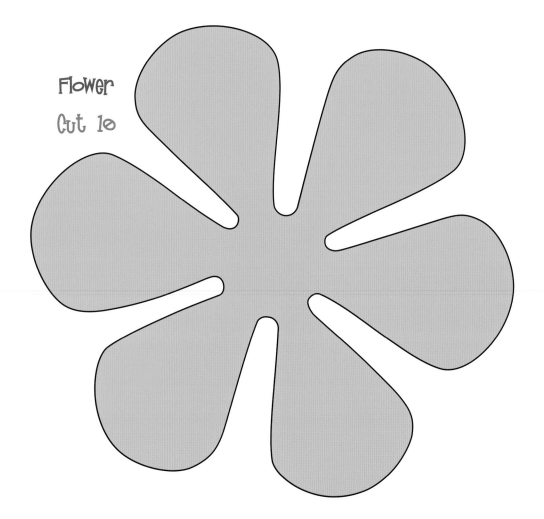

Flower
Cut 10

Give Peas a Chance Quilt

Give Peas a Chance Pillow

Finished size: approximately 20" x 20"

Fabric Requirements

Fabric A 3/4 yard pea focal for back and ruffle

Fabric B 5/8 yard white for front

Fabric C 7 polka dot fabrics, 1/4 yard of each for ruffle, loop closures, and buttons

Fabric D 1/2 yard polka dot for bias tape and back strip

Fabric E 8" x 8" square for flower appliqué

Batting 20-1/2" x 20-1/2" square

Lightweight fusible interfacing

6, 1-1/2"-diameter covered button forms

20" pillow form

Cutting Guide

Fabric A:
- Cut 1 rectangle 18" x 20-1/2" for left back
- Cut 1 rectangle 13" x 20-1/2" for right back
- Cut 3, 4" x 22" strips for ruffle

Fabric B:
- Cut 1 square 20-1/2" x 20-1/2"

Fabric C:
- Cut 7, 4" x 22-1/2" strips in 7 colors for ruffle
- Cut 5, 1-1/2" x 6" strips in 5 colors for loop closures
- Cut 6, 2-1/2" x 2-1/2" squares in 6 colors for buttons

Fabric D:
- Cut enough 3/4"-wide bias strips to equal 110"
- Cut 1 strip 2" x 20-1/2"

Fusible Interfacing:
- Cut 2 strips 3" x 20-1/2"
- Cut 6, 2-1/2" x 2-1/2" squares

Pillow Front

1. Trace the flower template on page 35 onto fusible web. Cut the shape out approximately 1/8" ouside the traced lines. Press fusible web shape, paper side up, onto the wrong side of the Fabric E square. Cut out the appliqué shape on the drawn line.

2. Center the appliqué shape on the Fabric B 20-1/2" x 20-1/2" square pillow front. Fuse in place.

3. Appliqué using your method of choice.
Note: Invisible thread was used to sew very close to the raw edge of the flower and then a scant 1/8" inside the flower's edge.

4. Use a fabric marking pen to draw 7-1/4", 10-1/4", and 13-1/4"-diameter circles centered on the pillow front around the flower appliqué.

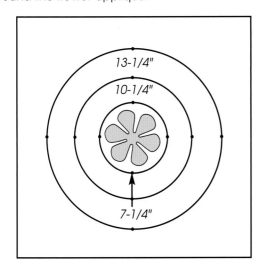

5. Center the pillow front on the 20-1/2" x 20-1/2" batting square; baste 1/2" from pillow front edges. Machine quilt 1/8" to 1/4" outside appliquéd flower.

6. Sew short ends of 3/4"-wide bias strips together to form one long strip. Press under 1/8" on the long edges of bias strip to make 1/2"-wide bias tape.

7. For pleated ruffles, sew short ends of Fabric A and Fabric C 4" x 22" strips together to form circles, using 4 strips for the outer ruffle and 3 strips for the middle ruffle. Sew ends of the remaining 3 strips together to make a long strip for the inner ruffle; this will be trimmed to fit later. Press each in half lengthwise with wrong sides together. In addition, press under 1/2" on one short end of inner ruffle strip.

8. Machine sew gathering stitches through both layers of each ruffle 1/4" from raw edges. Pull thread to slightly gather each ruffle. Refer to Gathering on page 11.

9. Beginning at the outer circle, sew the corresponding ruffle to the pillow top. Align the raw edges of the ruffle with the drawn circle and fold 1/2" pleats in the ruffle approximately every 1" to fit the ruffle to the circle as you sew.

10. Position bias tape from Step 6 over the raw edge of the outer ruffle, trimming tape so the ends overlap with the top end folded under. Sew in place with a narrow zigzag stitch along both long edges.

11. Repeat Steps 9 and 10 for the middle and inner ruffle. For the inner ruffle, trim the excess strip to fit, tucking the trimmed end inside the pressed end.

Pillow Back

1. Fuse 3" x 20-1/2" strips of interfacing along one 20-1/2" edge of the Fabric A 18" x 20-1/2" left back rectangle and the Fabric A 13" x 20-1/2" right back rectangle. Narrowly hem these edges and fold over 2-1/2"; press.

2. Press under 3/8" on both long edges of each Fabric C 1-1/2" x 6" strip. Press strips in half lengthwise with wrong sides together; sew. Strips should now measure approximately 3/8" x 6".

3. Fold strips in half to make loop closures and baste in place on the right side of left back rectangle. Beginning at the center, position a loop closure with ends 1-1/2" from the pressed edge. Continue working outward with loops 2-5/8" apart.

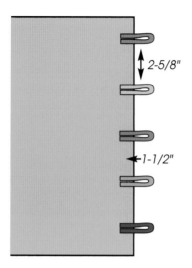

2-5/8"

←1-1/2"

4. Press under 1/2" on the long edges of the Fabric D 2" x 20-1/2" strip. Position on left back rectangle 3/4" from pressed edge, covering the ends of the loop closures. Sew close to both long edges of strip.

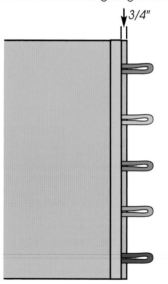

↓3/4"

Assembly of Pillow

1. Pin left back to pillow front with right sides together, aligning the raw edges of left back with 3 edges of front. Pin right back to pillow in the same manner; left and right backs will overlap approximately 4-1/2". Use a 1/2" seam allowance to sew backs to front. Trim corners. Turn pillow cover right side out through back opening.

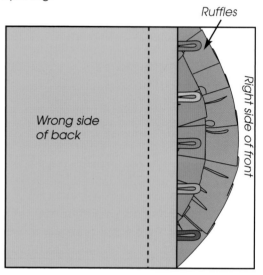

Ruffles

Wrong side of back

Right side of front

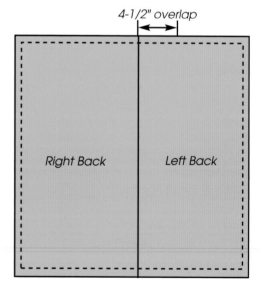

4-1/2" overlap

Right Back   Left Back

2. Fuse 2-1/2" x 2-1/2" squares of interfacing to wrong side of Fabric C 2-1/2" x 2-1/2" squares. Use these to cover button forms, following the manufacturer's instructions.

3. Sew 1 covered button on the pillow front centered on the appliquéd flower. Sew 5 covered buttons on the right pillow back in line with the loop closures.

4. Insert 20" pillow form through back opening. Button to close.

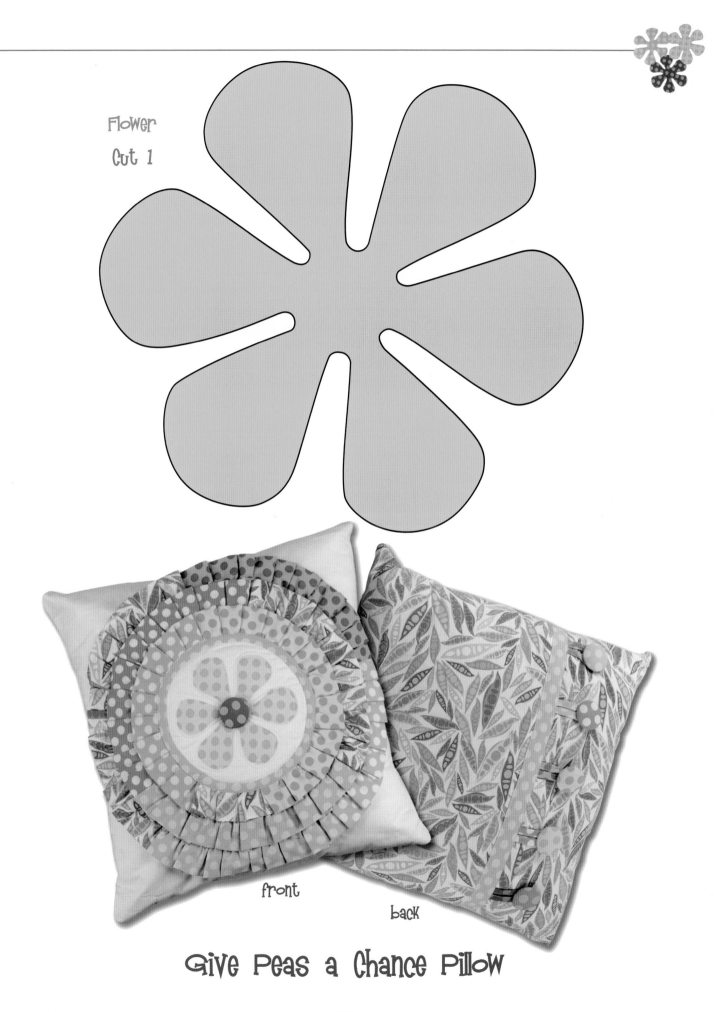

Flower
Cut 1

front

back

Give Peas a Chance Pillow

Give Peas a Chance
Table Runner

Finished size: approximately 14·1/2" x 42·1/2"

Two Sisters Tip

Lay out flowers as desired and take a photo of the placement so you won't forget the order. Use an appliqué sheet to press the flowers together before placement on the center square.

Fabric Requirements

Fabric A	1-5/8 yards pea focal for half-square triangles and backing
Fabric B	3/4 yard white for center square and binding
Fabric C	4 polka dot fabrics, 1/4 yard of each for half-square triangles
Fabric D	2, 8" x 8" squares in 2 colors for flower appliqués
Fabric E	3, 6" x 6" squares in 3 colors for flower appliqués
Batting	20" x 48"

Lightweight fusible web

Cutting Guide

Fabric A:
- Cut 2 strips 5" x WOF
  Sub cut into 16 squares 5" x 5"
- Cut 1 piece 20" x 48"

Fabric B:
- Cut 1 square 14-1/2" x 14-1/2"
- Cut 3 strips 2-1/4" x WOF for binding

Fabric C:
- Cut 1 strip 5" x WOF from each of the 4 fabrics
  Sub cut into 4 squares 5" x 5" for a total of 16 squares

Center square Appliqué

1. Trace 1 of each Flower A, B, C, D and E template on pages 38 - 40 onto fusible web. Cut the shapes out approximately 1/8" outside the traced lines. Press fusible web shapes, paper side up, onto the wrong side of the Fabric D and Fabric E squares. Cut out the appliqué shapes on the drawn lines.

2. Position the appliqué shapes on the Fabric B 14-1/2" x 14-1/2" square, referring to the photograph on page 40 for placement. Fuse in place.

3. Appliqué using your method of choice.
   Note: Invisible thread was used to buttonhole-stitch over the raw edges of each flower.

Half-square Triangles

1. Draw a diagonal line from corner to corner on the wrong side of the Fabric A 5" x 5" squares.

2. Place a Fabric A 5" x 5" square on a Fabric C 5" x 5" square, RST and aligning the edges. Sew 1/4" on either side of the drawn line. Cut on the drawn line to make 2 half-square triangles. Press seam to the dark fabric and trim to 4" x 4".

3. Repeat Step 2 to make 8 half-square triangles of each of the Fabric A/C combinations for a total of 32 half-square triangles.

Assembly

1. Sew together 8 same-color half-square triangles to make 2 rows as shown. Press seams in opposite directions. Join the rows to make a zigzag unit. Repeat to make 4 zigzag units, 1 of each Fabric A/C color combination.

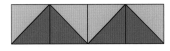

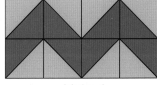

Make 4

2. Sew the zigzag units together in pairs for the end units. Press seams in one direction.

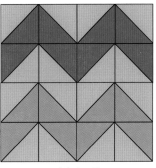

Make 2

3. Join the end units to opposite edges of the appliquéd Fabric B center square. Press seams away from the center.

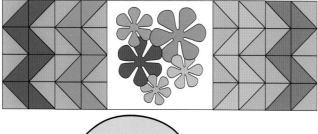

Finishing

1. Refer to General Instructions – Backing and Assembling the Layers on page 13.

2. Quilt as desired.

3. Refer to General Instructions – Binding on page 13 to bind the table runner using the Fabric B 2-1/4" x WOF strips.

Flowers

Cut 1 of each

A

B

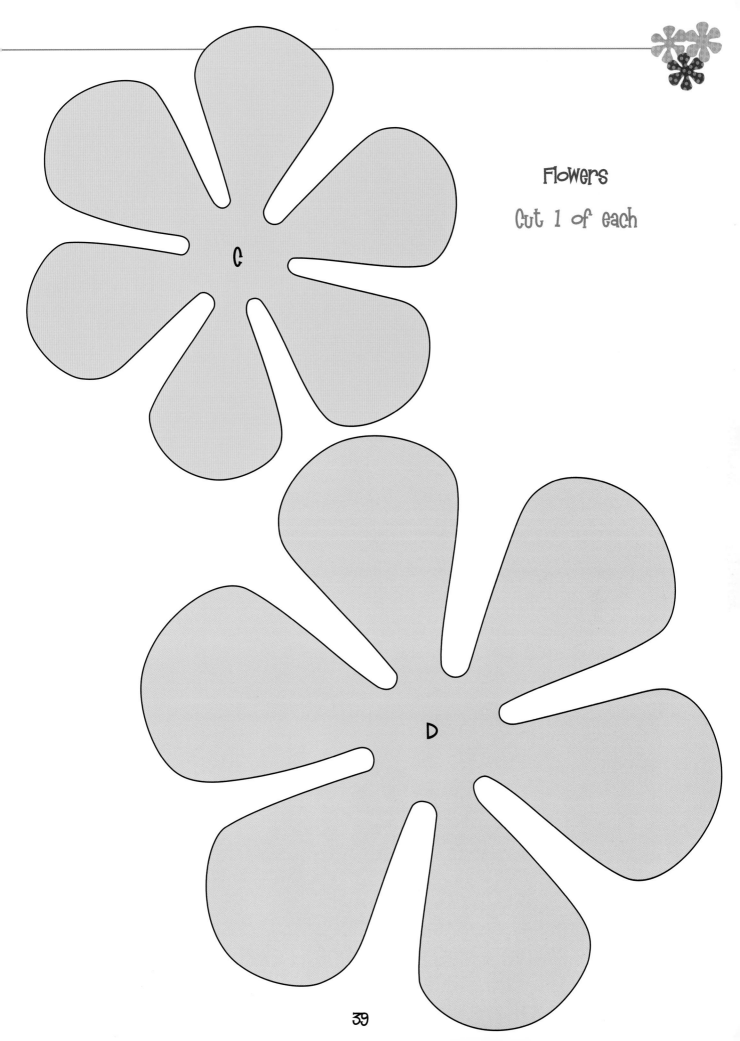

Flowers
Cut 1 of each

C

D

39

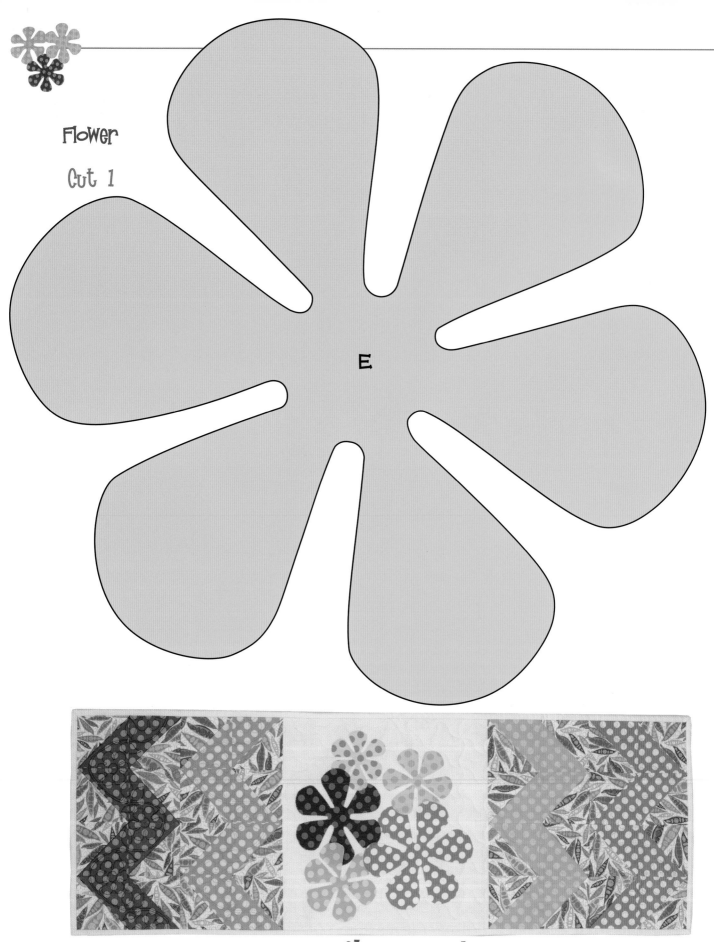

Flower

Cut 1

E

Give Peas a Chance Table Runner

Give Peas a Chance Napkin

Finished size: 15-1/2" x 15-1/2"

Makes 1 napkin

Fabric Requirements

Fabric A   16-1/2" x 16-1/2" square white

Fabric B   1-5/8" x WOF pea focal for ruffle

Fabric C   5" x 10" rectangle polka dot for flower appliqué

Heavyweight fusible web
        5" x 5" square

Assembly

1. Narrowly hem the long edges of the Fabric B 1-5/8" x WOF strip; the strip should measure approximately 1"-wide. Machine-baste down the center of the strip. Pull basting threads, gathering the fabric strip to make a ruffle approximately 28" long.

2. Pin the ruffle on the right side of the Fabric A 16-1/2" x 16-1/2" square with the center of the ruffle 2-1/2" from 2 edges of the square. Sew the ruffle to the square, stitching over the basting stitches.

3. To hem napkin, press under 1/4" twice along all edges, including the short edges of the ruffle in the hem. Sew close to the inner fold.

4. Fold a Fabric C 5" x 10" rectangle in half with wrong sides together to make a 5" x 5" square. To stiffen fabric, insert a 5" x 5" square of heavyweight fusible web between the fabric layers and fuse. Trace flower template A on page 38 onto one side of stiffened fabric and satin-stitch just inside traced line. Trim away fabric beyond satin stitching.

5. Position the flower on the napkin referring to photograph for placement. Secure the flower in place, sewing from the center of the flower outward in a circular motion.

Green Thumb Quilt

Whether you have a green thumb for a garden or nimble fingers for a quilt, the premise is the same. Our fingers are an extension of our hearts and minds creativeness. Give yourself permission to play, explore and create! Step outside the box and try a panel print and borders. You may just find your green thumb after all.

Finished size: approximately 51-1/2" x 51-1/2"

Fabric Requirements

Fabric A	panel print OR 2/3 yards fabric of choice for Center blocks
Fabric B	6 assorted prints, 1/3 yard of each for Outer blocks
Fabric C	2 yards border print for blocks
Fabric D	1-1/4 yards polka dot for border, binding, and ruffle
Fabric E	3-1/4 yards backing
Batting	58" x 58" square

Cutting Guide

Fabric A:
- Cut 9 squares 5-1/2" x 5-1/2" for Center block squares

Fabric B:
- Cut 1-2 strips 2-1/2" x WOF from 6 assorted prints for a total of 9 strips
  Sub cut a set of 2 strips 2-1/2" x 5-1/2" and 2 strips 2-1/2" x 9-1/2" from each strip for a total of 9 block frame sets
- Cut 2-3 squares 5-1/2" x 5-1/2" from each of the 6 fabrics for a total of 16 block squares

Fabric C:
- Cut 8 strips 2-1/2" x LOF, centering a border print in each strip
  Sub cut 16 matching sets of 2 strips 2-1/2" x 5-1/2" and 2 strips 2-1/2" x 9-1/2" for block frames

Fabric D:
- Cut 5 strips 3-1/2" x WOF for border
- Cut 6 strips 2-1/4" x WOF for binding
- Cut 5 strips 1-3/4" x WOF for ruffle

Framed square Blocks

1. For 1 block you will need 1 Fabric A 5-1/2" x 5-1/2" block square and 1 Fabric B matching block frame set of 2 strips 2-1/2" x 5-1/2" and 2 strips 2-1/2" x 9-1/2".

2. Sew 2 strips 2-1/2" x 5-1/2" to opposite sides of the 5-1/2" block square. Press seams toward strips. If the fabric is directional, as shown, sew these strips to the top and bottom edges of 5 block squares and to the side edges of 4 block squares.

Make 5 *Make 4*

3. Sew 2 strips 2-1/2" x 9-1/2" to the remaining two edges of the block square. Press seams toward strips. Make 9 Center blocks.

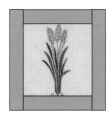

4. Repeat Steps 1-3 using the Fabric B, assorted print, 5-1/2" x 5-1/2" block squares and the Fabric C, assorted border print, 2-1/2" x 5-1/2" and 2-1/2" x 9-1/2" block frame strips. Make 16 Outer blocks.

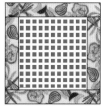

Make 16 Outer blocks

Assembly

1. Lay out 9 Center and 16 Outer blocks in 5 rows of 5 blocks, alternating the direction of the blocks in a checkerboard pattern as shown. By rotating the blocks in this fashion, the seams will meet only at the block corners, not along the block edges.

2. Sew together one row at a time. Press seams in opposite directions for each row. Sew rows together to make the quilt center.

Borders

Note: If you wish to miter your borders, refer to Mitered Borders on page 12.

1. Piece the Fabric D 3-1/2" x WOF border strips to make the following: 2, 3-1/2" x 45-1/2" side borders and 2, 3-1/2" x 51-1/2" top and bottom borders.

2. Sew Fabric D 3-1/2" x 45-1/2" border strips to the sides of the quilt center. Press seams toward border.

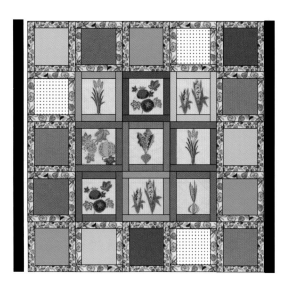

3. Sew Fabric D 3-1/2" x 51-1/2" border strips to the top and bottom edges of the quilt center. Press seams toward border.

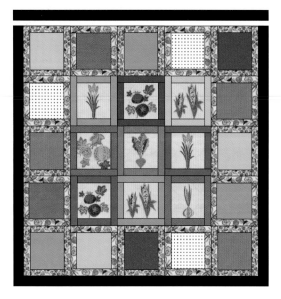

Finishing

1. Refer to General Instructions – Backing and Assembling the Layers on page 13.

2. Quilt as desired.

3. Refer to General Instructions – Binding on page 13 to bind the quilt using the Fabric D 2-1/4" x WOF strips.

Ruffle

Note: The ruffle is added after the quilt is quilted.

1. Sew short ends of the Fabric D 1-3/4" x WOF ruffle strips together to form one long strip. Press seams open.

2. Turn under each long edge of strip 1/4" and then 1/4" again; press. The strip should measure about 3/4" wide. Sew close to the inner folds.

See Two Sisters Tip - Got to have Tools! on page 11.

3. Machine baste down the center of the strip. Pull basting threads, gathering the fabric strip evenly to make a ruffle approximately 3 yards (108" long).

4. Pin the ruffle on the front of the quilt along the seams of the 9 Center blocks. Adjust the gathers to fit evenly; turn under the raw ends. Sew the ruffle to the quilt, stitching over the basting stitches.

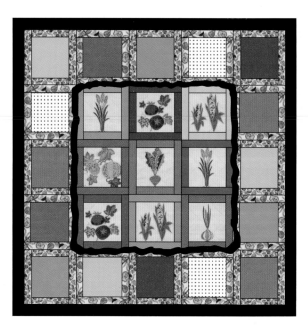

44

Green Thumb Quilt

45

Green Thumb
Radish Table Runner

Finished size: approximately 20" x 28"

Fabric Requirements

Fabric A   1/8 yard each of 5 assorted prints for leaves

Fabric B   3/4 yard of green print for leaves and leaf backing

Fabric C   1/2 yard of red-and-white print for radish

Fabric D   3/4 yard of red-on-red print for radishes

Lightweight batting

Cutting Guide

Fabric A:
- Cut 1 strip 3-1/4" x WOF from each of 5 assorted fabrics
  Sub cut each strip into 3 rectangles 3-1/4" x 12" for a total of 15 strips for leaf fronts

Fabric B:
- Cut 7 strips 3-1/4" x WOF
  Sub cut into 21 rectangles 3-1/4" x 12"; 3 for leaf front and 18 for leaf backs

Fabric C:
- Cut 1 radish using template on page 49
- Cut 2 rectangles 7-1/4" x 14" for radish back

Fabric D:
- Cut 2 radishes using template on page 49
- Cut 4 rectangles 7-1/4" x 14" for radish back

Batting:
- Cut 3 radishes using template on page 49
- Cut 9 rectangles 6" x 12" for leaves

Leaves

1. Sew the Fabric A and Fabric B 3-1/4" x 12" leaf front rectangles together in pairs. Press seams open.

Make 9

2. Sew the Fabric B 3-1/4" x 12" leaf back rectangles together in pairs, leaving a 2" opening in the center. Press seams open. Use the leaf templates on page 49 to cut 3 of each leaf from the pairs, positioning the templates on the right side of the back fabric with the back openings near the vertical center of the leaf backs.

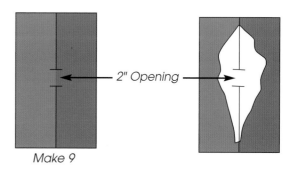

Make 9

3. Position a leaf front pair right side up on a 6" x 12" batting rectangle. Place a leaf back right side down on the leaf front. Leaves are intentionally off-center over the fabrics. Refer to the photo on page 48 as a guide in positioning the leaf back over the seam of the leaf front; pin. Sew layers together 1/4" from edges of leaf back. Trim batting and clip seam. Turn right side out through center back opening. Press; slipstitch the opening closed.

4. Repeat Step 3 to make 9 leaves. Quilt leaves as desired.

5. Make sets of 3 leaves, using 1 of each shape. Position the leaves so they touch along the lower side edges and overlap at the middle. Sew the leaves together about 1/2" from the bottom edges and edge-stitch the area that overlaps.

Radishes

1. Sew the Fabric C 7-1/4" x 14" back rectangles together on a long edge, leaving a 3" opening in the center. Press seam open. Use the radish template on page 49 to cut the radish back, aligning the vertical center of the template with the back seam.

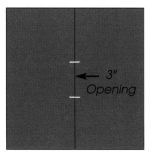
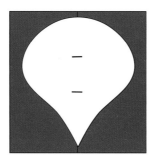

2. Position the Fabric C radish front right side up on a radish batting; baste together 1/4" from edges. Place a leaf set right side down on the radish front with the bottom ends extending approximately 1/4" beyond the top of the radish. Sew to secure along the basting line. Fold in the leaves and pin to keep them away from the radish's seam allowance.

3. Place the radish back right side down on the radish front with the leaf set sandwiched between. Sew layers together, catching the bottom ends of the leaves in the stitching. Trim batting and clip seam. Turn right side out through center back opening. Remove pins from leaves. Press; slipstitch the opening closed.

4. Repeat Steps 1-3 using the 4 Fabric D 7-1/4" x 14" rectangles and 2 Fabric D radish fronts to make 2 additional radishes. Quilt horizontal lines across each radish 1-1/2" to 2-1/2" apart.

5. Referring to the photo, place the 3 radishes right side down on a flat surface. Hand sew the radishes together where they touch.

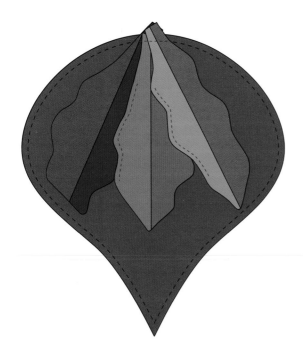

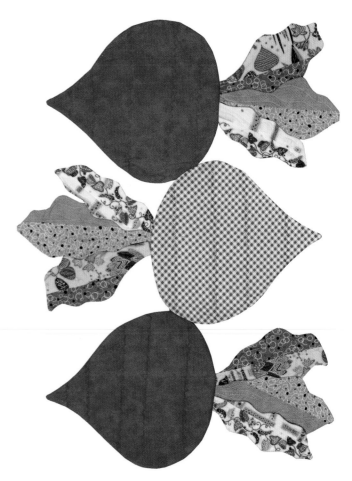

Radish Table Runner

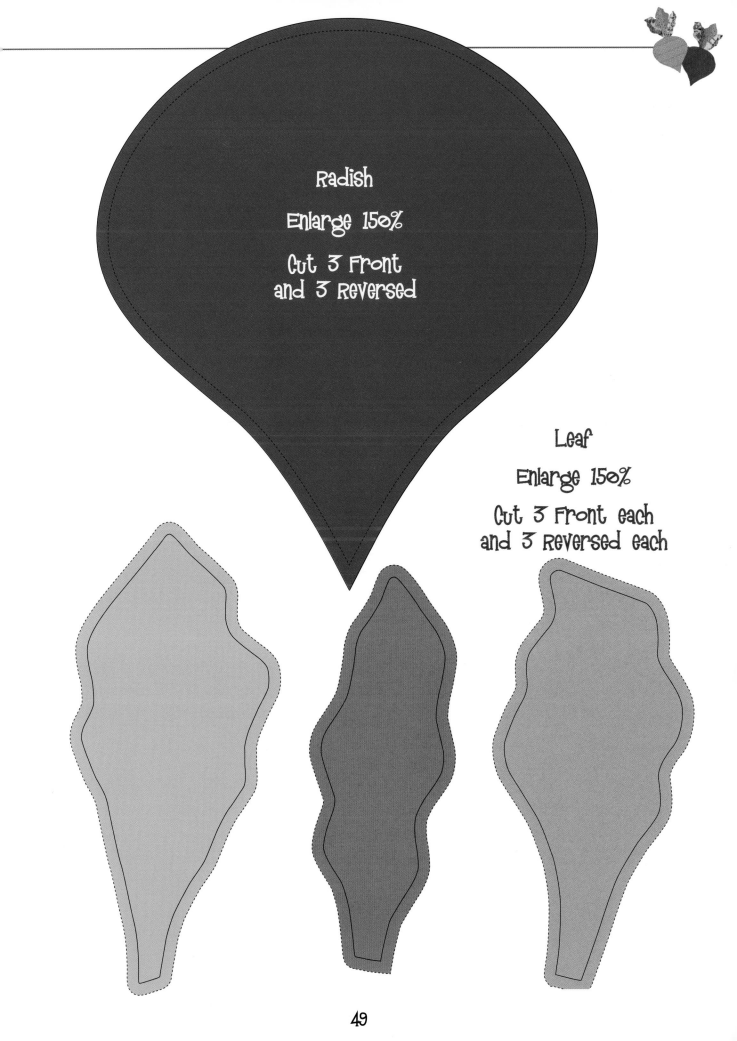

Radish

Enlarge 150%

Cut 3 Front
and 3 Reversed

Leaf

Enlarge 150%

Cut 3 Front each
and 3 Reversed each

Green Thumb Place Mat

Makes 1 place mat

Fabric Requirements

Fabric A	6 assorted prints, 1/4 yard or 1 fat quarter of each
Fabric B	1/4 yard polka dot
Fabric C	5/8 yard green print for binding, backing, and triangles
Fabric D	1/8 yard red print for ruffle
Batting	18" x 24" rectangle

Cutting Guide

Fabric A:
• Cut 16 triangles from the assorted fabrics using template on page 51

Fabric B:
• Cut 1 strip 2-1/2" x WOF
    Sub cut 2 strips 2-1/2" x 14" for border
• Cut 3 triangles using template on page 5

Fabric C:
• Cut 2 strips 2-1/4" x WOF for binding
• Cut 1 rectangle 18" x 24" for backing
• Cut 2 triangles using template on page 5

Fabric D:
• Cut 2 strips 1-3/4" x 28" for ruffle

Finished place mat: approximately 19-1/2" x 14"

Assembly

1. Lay out the 21 triangles in 3 rows of 7 triangles, alternating the direction of the triangles as shown.

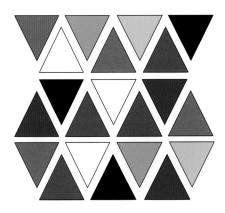

2. Sew the triangles in each row together; press. Join rows to make the place mat center. Press seams in one direction.

3. Trim the side edges of the place mat center 1/4" beyond the triangle points.

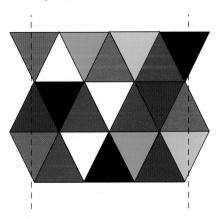

4. Sew Fabric B 2-1/2" x 14" border strips to the sides of the place mat center. Press seams toward border.

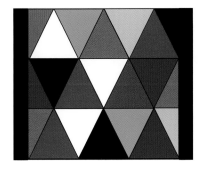

Finishing

1. Refer to General Instructions – Backing and Assembling the Layers on page 13.

2. Quilt as desired.

Ruffle

1. Turn under each long edge of the Fabric D 1-3/4" x 28" ruffle strips 1/4" and then 1/4" again; press. The strips should measure about 3/4" wide. Sew close to the inner folds.

See Two Sisters Tip - Got to have Tools! on page 11.

2. Machine baste down the center of each strip. Pull basting threads, gathering the fabric strip evenly to make a ruffle approximately 14" long.

3. Pin the ruffles on the front of the place mat centered on the border seams. Adjust the gathers to fit evenly. Sew the ruffles to the place mat, stitching over the basting stitches.

Binding

Refer to General Instructions – Binding on page 13 to bind the place mat using the Fabric C 2-1/4" x WOF strips, including the short edges of the ruffle in the binding.

Triangle
Cut 21

Green Thumb Purse

Finished size: approximately 16" x 15" x 3-3/4"

Fabric Requirements

Fabric A	1 yard vegetable focal for front, back, and straps
Fabric B	1/2 yard green print for sides/bottom, and pocket lining
Fabric C	1-1/4 yards gray print for lining
Fabric D	1/8 yard of 6 assorted prints for pocket and flowers; Honey Bun strips or scraps can be used here
Fabric E	1-3/4" x 45" strip of border print for binding
Batting	2 yards

4 curtain grommets

1 yard, 3/8"-wide red-with-white grosgrain ribbon

Cutting Guide

Fabric A:
- Cut 2 rectangles 20" x 18" for front and back
- Cut 2 strips 5-1/2" x 42" for straps

Fabric B:
- Cut 1 strip 5-1/2" x 42" for sides/bottom
- Cut 1 pocket using template on page 55 for pocket lining

Fabric C:
- Cut 1 strip 7-1/2" x 44" for sides/bottom lining
- Cut 2 rectangles 22" x 20" for front and back lining

Fabric D:
- Cut 1 strip 1-3/4" x WOF from each of 2 assorted fabrics for a total of 2 flower strips
- Cut 1 strip 1-1/2"-1-3/4" x WOF from each of 5 assorted fabrics for a total of 5 pocket front strips

Batting:
- Cut 2 rectangles 22" x 20" for front and back
- Cut 2 strips 2" x 42" for straps
- Cut 1 strip 7-1/2" x 44" for sides/bottom
- Cut 1 pocket using template on page 55

Prepare Purse Fabric

1. Use chalk or water-soluble marker to draw vertical lines on the Fabric A 20" x 18" front and back rectangles. Space the lines 1-3/8" apart.

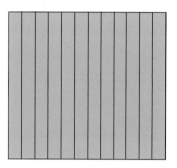

2. Lay a Fabric C 22" x 20" lining rectangle right side down on a flat surface. Center a 22" x 20" batting piece on the lining. Smooth the marked Fabric A front rectangle on the batting and pin or spray baste in place on the batting. Approximately 1" of batting and lining will extend beyond the edges of the front fabric. Sew on the drawn lines. Repeat for the back rectangle.

3. Repeat Steps 1 and 2 with the Fabric B 5-1/2" x 42" sides/bottom strip, Fabric C 7-1/2" x 44" lining strip, and 7-1/2" x 42" batting strip, drawing lines lengthwise on the Fabric B strip.

4. Use the template on page 55 to cut the purse front and back from the quilted fabric. Trim the quilted sides/bottom fabric to measure 4-1/4" x 40-1/2".

Pocket

1. Cut 12" lengths from the 5 Fabric D 1-1/2" – 1-3/4"-wide strips. With right sides facing, use a 1/4" seam allowance to sew these together in any order along the long edges to make a pieced fabric square that measures approximately 12" x 12". Press the seams in one direction. Use the template on page 55 to cut the pocket front, positioning the template on the pieced fabric so strips run diagonally across the pocket.

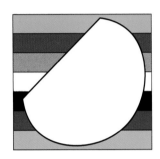

2. Position the pocket front right side up on the pocket batting. Smooth the Fabric B pocket lining right side down on the pocket front. Sew layers together, leaving a 3" opening at the top edge for turning. Trim batting and clip seam. Turn right side out. Press; slipstitch the opening closed.

3. For flowers, narrowly hem the long edges of the Fabric D 1-3/4" x WOF strips; the strips should measure about 1" wide. Hand sew basting stitches in a zigzag line down the length of each strip.

4. Working with one strip at a time, pull the basting thread to evenly gather the fabric strip. Wind the gathered strip into a circle on the pocket to form flower, hand-stitching in place as you go. Trim excess strip and knot end of basting thread to secure gathers. Make second flower with remaining strip.

Straps

1. Press under 1/2" on both long edges of a Fabric A 5-1/2" x 42" strap. Fold the strap in half lengthwise with a 2" x 42" batting strip between the layers. Repeat for the second strap.

2. Sew 1/8" from the long edges of both straps. Sew 2 additional lengthwise lines of stitching spaced 5/8" apart on each strap.

Assembly

1. Make darts in purse front and back.

2. Mark placement of grommets on purse front and back as indicated on template. Add grommets to front and back following manufacturer's instructions.

3. Center the pocket on the purse front 5-1/2" from the top edge and pin. Sew the pocket to the front a scant 1/4" from the side and bottom edges of the pocket.

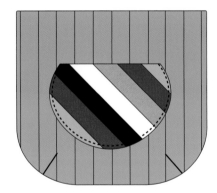

4. Pin the quilted sides/bottom piece to the purse front RST, easing to fit; sew. Sew the opposite edge of the sides/bottom strip to the purse back in the same manner. Turn purse right side out.

5. Press under 1/4" on one long edge of Fabric E 1-3/4" x 45" binding strip. Working on the lining side of purse, sew the opposite long edge of binding to purse. Trim and join ends of binding to fit. Fold binding over to the outside of purse and sew in place close to pressed edge.

6. Insert ends of one strap through grommets on purse front from the outside of the purse to the inside. Sew ends to strap about 1-1/2" above top of purse. Wrap a 9" length of 3/8"-wide ribbon around the strap to cover the stitching at each strap end. Hand sew ribbon end to secure. Repeat with second strap for purse back.

Pocket

Enlarge 155%

Cut 1 Pieced Fabric
Cut 1 Lining
Cut 1 Batting

1/4" seam allowance has been added

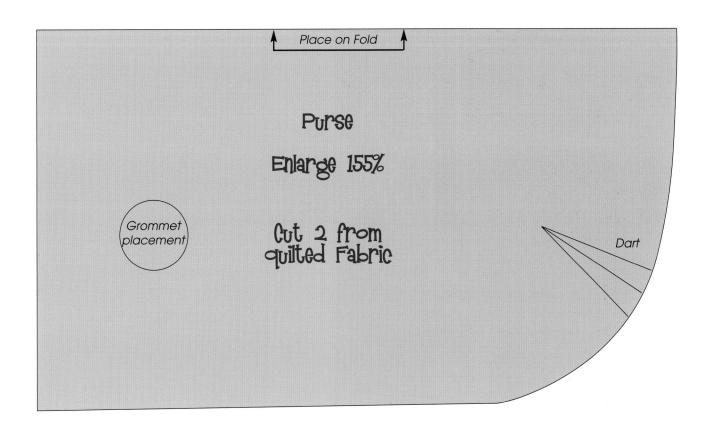

Place on Fold

Purse

Enlarge 155%

Cut 2 from
quilted Fabric

Grommet
placement

Dart

Green Thumb Hat

Fabric Requirements

*Fabric yardage required will be determined
by the size of hat needed.
Refer to the templates on page 58-59 for hat sizes.*

Fabric A   vegetable focal for top, crown, and brim

Fabric B   polka dot for brim lining

Fabric C   top and crown lining

Fabric D   1/6 yard red-on-red print for flower

3/4 yard of 1"-wide black grosgrain ribbon

Lightweight batting

Heavyweight interfacing

2"-diameter circle of black felt

Pin base

Fabric glue

Cutting Guide

Fabric A:
• Cut 1 rectangle 30" x 15" for top and crown
• Cut 1 brim using template on page 58

Fabric B:
• Cut 1 brim using template on page 58

Fabric C:
• Cut 1 rectangle 32" x 17" for lining

Fabric D:
* Cut 1 strip 4" x 42" for flower

Batting:
• Cut 1 rectangle 32" x 17"
• Cut 1 brim using template on page 58

Interfacing:
• Cut 1 brim using template on page 58

Prepare Fabric

1. Use chalk or water-soluble marker to draw diagonal lines on the Fabric A 30" x 15" rectangle. Space the lines 1-3/4" apart and at a 60-degree angle in both directions across the rectangle.

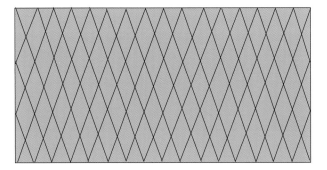

2. Lay the Fabric C 32" x 17" lining rectangle right side down on a flat surface. Place the 32" x 17" batting piece on the lining. Center and smooth the marked Fabric A rectangle on the batting and pin or spray baste in place on the batting. Approximately 1" of batting and lining will extend beyond the edges of the front fabric. Sew on the drawn lines.

3. Use the templates on pages 58-59 to cut the hat crown and hat top from the quilted fabric.

Assembly of Hat

Use a 5/8" seam allowance and sew with RST unless otherwise stated.

1. Overcast or zigzag-stitch the raw edges of the crown and top. Sew together the short edges of the crown, making a circle; this is the center back of hat. Press seam open. Sew the crown to the top.

2. Baste the brim interfacing to the wrong side of the Fabric A brim; sew the short edges together. Baste the brim batting to the wrong side of the Fabric B brim lining; sew the short edges together. Trim the batting from seam allowance. Press the seams open.

3. Pin the Fabric A brim to the brim lining along the outer edge with RST, aligning the seams. Sew, trim batting, and clip seam. Turn brim right side out and press.

4. Sew 4 rows of machine quilting around the brim, beginning 1/4" from the outer edge and spacing the lines 1" apart. Sew the brim to the bottom edge of the crown, aligning the seams at the center back.

5. Zigzag-stitch 1"-wide ribbon over the inside edge of the brim. Fold ribbon up to the crown and tack in place at the center back, center front, and once on each side.

Add Flower

1. Press under 1/2" on one short edge of the Fabric D 4" x 42" strip. Press the strip in half lengthwise; overcast or zigzag-stitch the long edges together. Sew a row of basting stitches a scant 1/4" from the long raw edge. Pull the basting thread to evenly gather the fabric strip.

2. With the folded edge at the top, fold down the remaining short edge of the fabric strip at a 45-degree angle so the short edge extends about 1/2" below the gathered edge.

3. Roll the fabric strip around the folded end 3 or 4 times, forming the center of the flower. Sew through the bottom several times to secure. Sew the bottom to the center of the 2"-diameter felt circle.

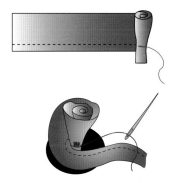

4. Continue wrapping the remaining fabric strip around the center of the flower for the outer petals, sewing the gathered edge to the felt as you go. Knot and glue the gathered edge of the flower to secure; let dry. Trim any excess from the felt circle.

5. Glue the pin to the opposite side of the felt circle. When dry, pin the flower to the hat crown.

Large

Medium

Small

Hat Brim

Enlarge 150%

Add 5/8" seam Allowance

Grainline

Place on Fold

Cut 1 Main Fabric
Cut 1 Lining
Cut 1 Lightweight Batting
Cut 1 Heavy Interfacing

Large

Medium

Small

Hat Crown

Enlarge 150%

Add 5/8" seam Allowance

Cut 1

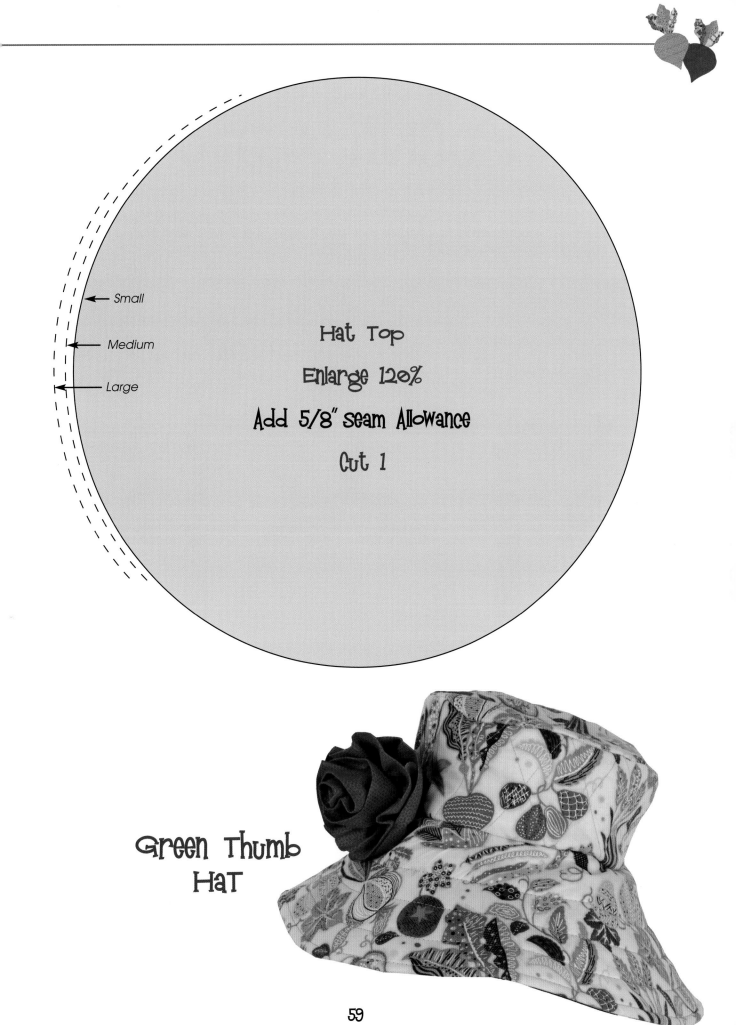

Small

Medium

Large

Hat Top

Enlarge 120%

Add 5/8" seam Allowance

Cut 1

Green Thumb
Hat

Punkin Quilt

When fall arrives I can feel the winds of change. The air is brisk and cool
even as the sun shines through the autumn canvas palettes golden glow.
This is a favorite time of year for me. The Punkin quilt will draw you in with
its harvest colors and, for me, is an expression of gratitude for all of life's bounty.

Finished size: approximately 42" x 42"

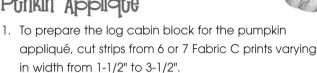

Fabric Requirements

Note: It is important to pre-starch your fabrics before beginning this quilt.

Fabric A   1 yard off-white for background and outer border

Fabric B   2/3 yard brown print for stem, inner border, and braided border

Fabric C   10 assorted orange prints, 1/4 yard of each for pumpkin appliqué, braided border, and corner stones; Honey Bun strips may be used here for quick assembly

Fabric D   2 assorted green prints, 1/4 yard each for leaf appliqués and braided border

Fabric E   3/8 yard of orange print for binding

Fabric F   2-2/3 yards backing OR 1-1/3 yards if using fabric with 44" of usable fabric without the selvages (but take care, it will be close)

Lightweight fusible web

Brown pearl cotton

Cutting Guide

Fabric A:
- Cut 1 square 21-1/2" x 21-1/2" for background
- Cut 4 strips 3" x WOF
  Sub cut into 4 strips 3" x 37" for outer border

Fabric B:
- Cut 4 strips 2-1/4" x WOF
  Sub cut into 2 strips 2-1/4" x 21-1/2" and 2 strips 2-1/4" x 25" for inner border
- Cut 3 strips 1-1/2" x WOF
  Sub cut into 21 rectangles 1-1/2" x 6" for braided border

Fabric C:
- Cut 3 strips 1-1/2" x WOF from each of the 10 fabrics for a total of 30 strips
  Sub cut each strip into 7 rectangles 1-1/2" x 6" for a total of 210 rectangles for braided border
- Cut 4 squares 3" x 3" from a dark orange print for corner squares
- Cut 1 rectangle 2-3/4" x 5-3/4" from a light orange print for pumpkin center

Fabric D:
- Cut 2 strips 1-1/2" x WOF from each of the 2 fabrics for a total of 4 strips
  Sub cut each strip into 7 rectangles 1-1/2" x 6" for a total of 28 rectangles for braided border

Fabric E:
- Cut 5 strips 2-1/4" x WOF for binding

Punkin Appliqué

1. To prepare the log cabin block for the pumpkin appliqué, cut strips from 6 or 7 Fabric C prints varying in width from 1-1/2" to 3-1/2".

2. Sew one strip to a short edge of the Fabric C 2-3/4" x 5-3/4" light orange print rectangle. Trim the strip even with the adjacent edge of the rectangle. Press seam away from rectangle.

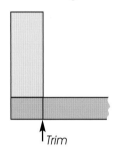

Trim

3. Continue adding strips outward from the rectangle in this manner until the log cabin block measures approximately 11" x 15".

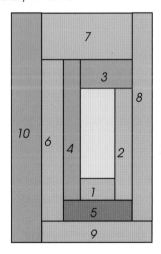

4. Cut a 3-1/2" x 15" strip from 2 Fabric C dark orange prints and add a strip to the side edges. Press seams away from center.

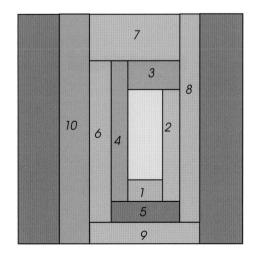

5. Trace one pumpkin from the template on page 64 onto fusible web. Cut the shape out approximately 1/8" outside the traced line. Cut away the center of the pumpkin shape, cutting about 1" inside the traced line. Press fusible web shape, paper side up, onto the wrong side of the log cabin block being careful not to distort the block. Cut out the appliqué shape on the drawn line.

6. Position the pumpkin shape on the Fabric A 21-1/2" x 21-1/2" square, referring to the photograph on page 67 for placement. Fuse in place. Appliqué using your method of choice. A decorative stitch and contrasting thread were used on the project shown.

7. Trace one stem and one of each leaf from the templates on pages 65-66 onto fusible web. Cut the shapes out approximately 1/8" outside the traced lines. Press fusible web shapes, paper side up, onto the wrong side of leftover Fabric B and Fabric D scraps. Cut out the appliqué shapes on the drawn lines.

8. Position the stem and leaf shapes and fuse in place. Appliqué using your method of choice.

9. Use brown pearl cotton to embroider tendrils, referring to the photograph on page 65.

Borders

1. Sew 2 Fabric B 2-1/4" x 21-1/2" inner border strips to the top and bottom edges of the appliquéd quilt center. Press seams toward border.

2. Sew 2 Fabric B 2-1/4" x 25" inner border strips to the side edges of the quilt center. Press seams toward border.

Two Sisters Tip

Place strips in a brown paper bag & mix them up. Draw strips out randomly. This takes the pressure out of choosing fabrics and makes your braid strips a real potluck!

3. Use the 1-1/2" x 6" rectangles from Fabric B, C and D to make the braided middle border. With RST, sew the end of one 6" strip to another using a scant 1/4" seam.

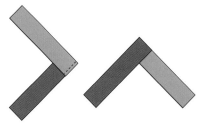

4. Line up another strip even with the left hand side and stitch from top to bottom using a 1/4" seam. Continue to add strips in this manner, building one upon another until it is long enough to cut a 24-1/2" length of braid.

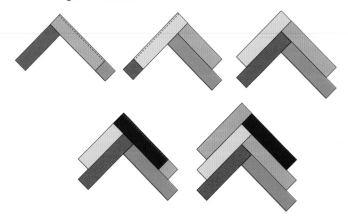

5. Trim the braid off on both sides to make it 6-1/2" wide by using a long ruler and finding roughly the center of the braid. Line the ruler up at the 3-1/4" mark. Using a rotary cutter, trim off one side of the braid. Repeat on the other side making sure the braid is 6-1/2" wide. The braid strip should measure 6-1/2" x 24-1/2".

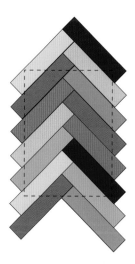

6. Repeat Steps 3-5 to make a second 24-1/2" side border and two 37" top and bottom borders.

7. Sew the two 24-1/2" braided borders to the side edges of the quilt. Press seams away from center. Sew the two 37" braided borders to the top and bottom edges and press seam away from center.

8. Sew 2 Fabric A 3" x 37" outer border strips to opposite edges of the quilt. Press seams toward outer border.

9. Sew Fabric C 3" x 3" corner squares to each end of the remaining Fabric A 3" x 37" outer border strips. Press seams toward border strips. Sew these to the remaining edges of the quilt. Press seams toward outer border.

Finishing

1. Refer to General Instructions – Backing and Assembling the Layers on page 13.

2. Quilt as desired.

3. Refer to General Instructions – Binding on page 13 to bind the quilt using the Fabric E 2-1/4" x WOF strips.

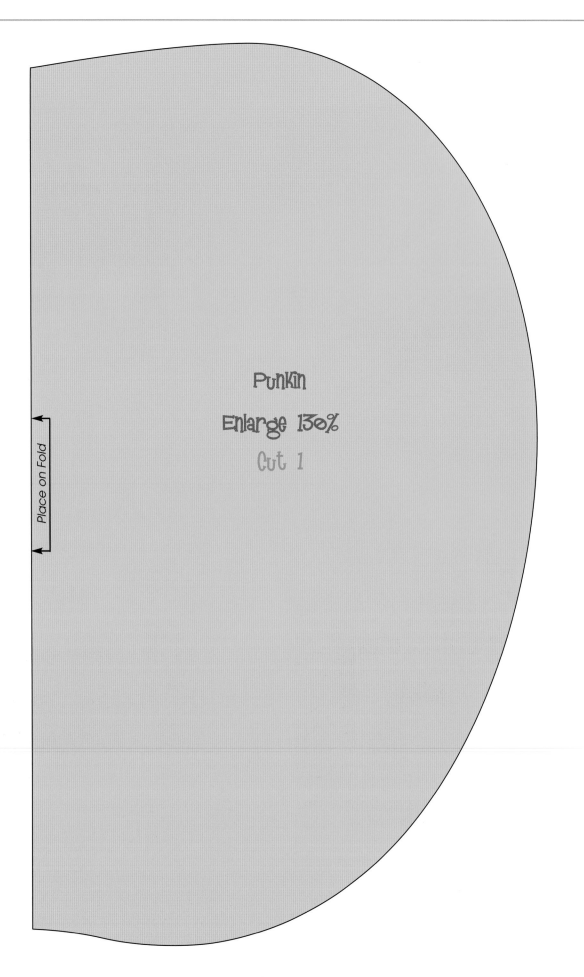

Punkin

Enlarge 130%

Cut 1

Place on Fold

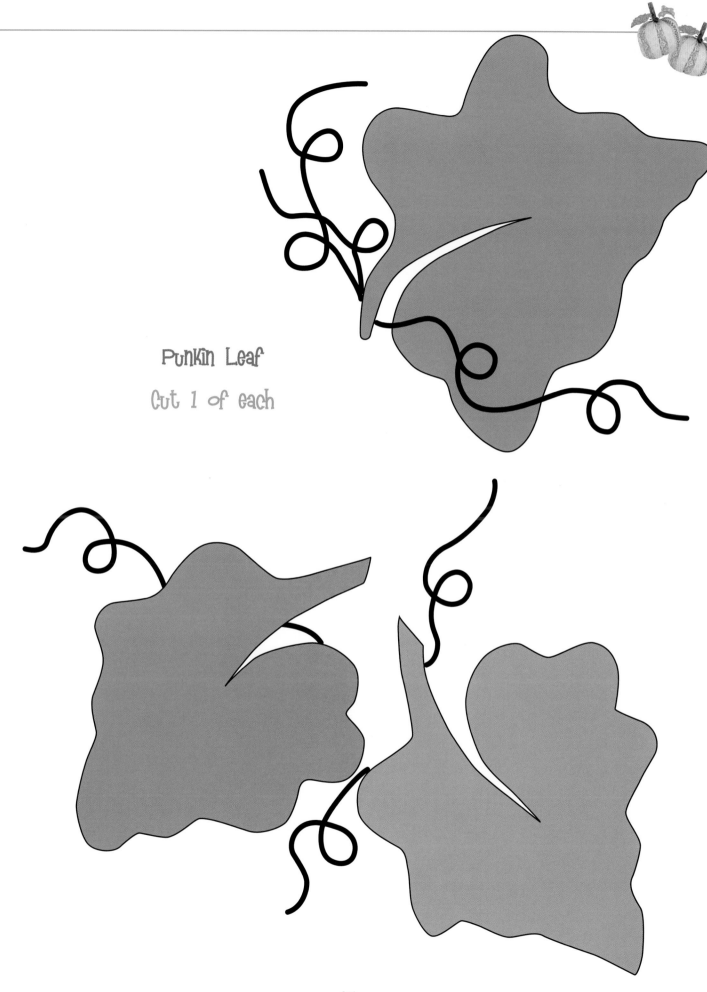

Punkin Leaf

Cut 1 of each

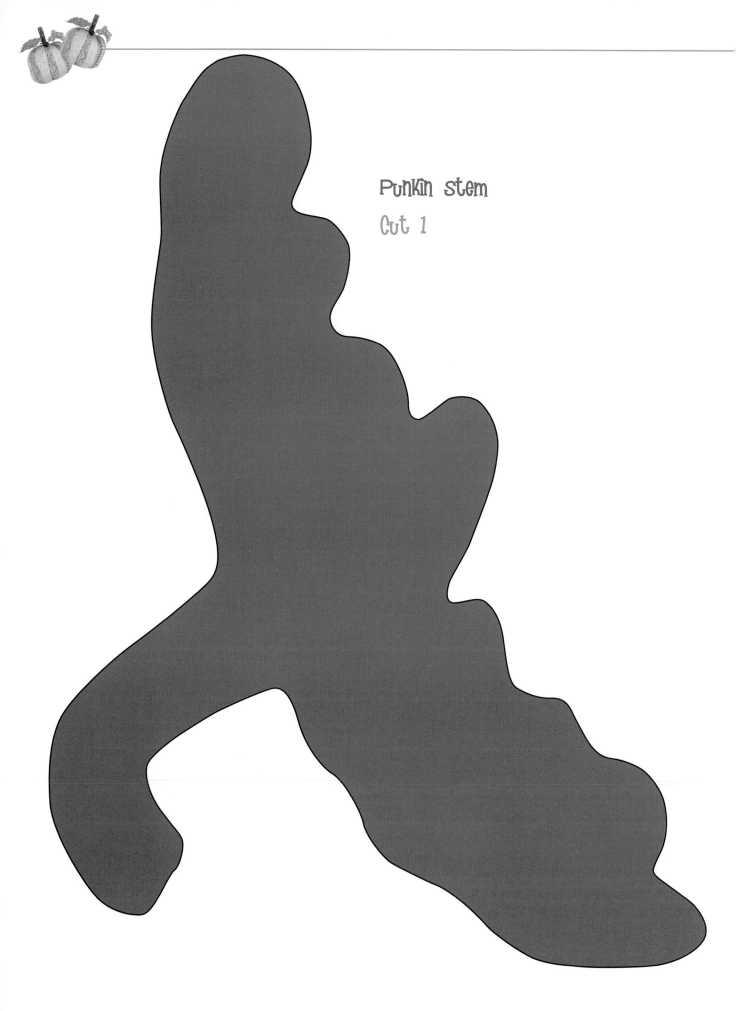

Punkin stem
Cut 1

Punkin Quilt

Punkin Purse

Finished size: approximately 16" x 10" x 6"

Fabric Requirements

Fabric A Fat quarter or 1/3 yard print for center front and back and small pocket

Fabric B 1/3 yard print for side and lining

Fabric C 1/3 yard print for side and lining

Fabric D Fat quarter or 1/3 yard print for lining

Fabric E 11" x 12" rectangle of print for large pocket

Medium-weight iron-on interfacing

2-1/2 yards 1-1/2"-wide webbing

Magnetic snap closure

Two 1-1/4"-diameter buttons

Pearl cotton

6" square of off-white fabric

Cutting Guide

Fabric A:
• Cut 2 centers using template on page 71
• Cut 1 rectangle 6" x 8" for small pocket

Fabric B:
• Cut 2 sides and 2 sides reversed using template on page 71

Fabric C:
• Cut 2 sides and 2 sides reversed using template on page 71

Fabric D:
• Cut 2 centers using template on page 71

Iron-on Interfacing:
• Cut 2 centers using template on page 71
• Cut 2 sides and 2 sides reversed using template on page 71
• Cut 2-3/4" x 1-1/4" rectangle

Webbing:
• Cut 2 lengths 29-1/2" for outside and inside bands
• Cut 2 lengths 28" for straps

Pockets

1. Press under 1/2" on both 8" edges of the Fabric A small pocket rectangle and on both 12" edges of the Fabric E large pocket rectangle.

2. Fold the rectangles in half with wrong sides together to make a 4" x 5" rectangle and a 6" x 10" rectangle. Sew together the raw edges of each rectangle with a 3/8" seam allowance to form a tube. Turn the tubes right side out and press, centering the seam on one side of each pocket.

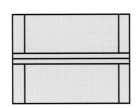 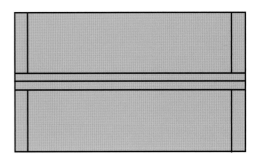

Assembly of Purse and Lining

1. Fuse the appropriate iron-on interfacing piece to the wrong side of 2 Fabric A centers, 1 Fabric B side and side reversed, and 1 Fabric C side and side reversed.

2. Sew a Fabric B and Fabric C side piece onto the long edges of a Fabric A center for purse front. Press seams away from the center. Top-stitch side pieces 1/4" from seam. Repeat for purse back.

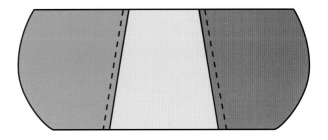

3. Sew the purse front to the purse back, leaving the top edge open.

4. To box the bottom of the purse, work with the purse inside out and one corner at a time. Bring the bottom corner of the purse to the center/side seam to make a fold in the bottom of the side pieces, keeping the bottom seam aligned.

5. Measure 1-1/2" from the fold at the seam. Draw a slightly curved line across bottom at this measurement and pin in place. Make sure the ends of the line are approximately 2" from the seam. Sew on line. Trim seam to 3/8" and overcast edges. Repeat for the remaining corner. Turn purse right side out.

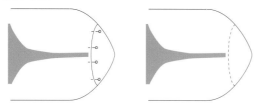

6. Make the pleats along the top edge of the purse front and back as indicated on the side template. Sew in place.

7. Sew the lining pieces together, following Step 2 and omitting the top stitching. Center the small pocket, seam side down, on the center piece of the front lining 4" below top edge. Sew along the side and bottom edges. Center the large pocket, seam side down, on the back lining 3" below top edge. Sew along the side and bottom edges and down the center of the pocket, dividing it in two.

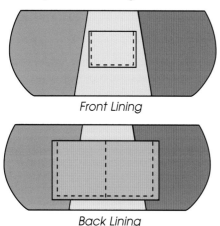

Front Lining

Back Lining

8. Complete the lining, following Steps 3-6; do not turn. Insert the lining into purse with wrong sides together; baste the top edges together with a 1/2" seam allowance.

9. Pin a 29-1/2" length of webbing around the top of purse for outside band. Position band to cover the basting stitches, beginning with one end at a side seam and folding under the opposite end to overlap the first. Sew in place close to the bottom edge of band.

10. Pin a 28" strap on the purse front with the ends near the basting stitches of lining and align the strap with the center/side seams of purse. Sew in place along top edge of outside band. Repeat for second strap on purse back.

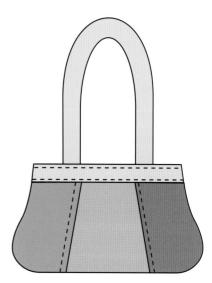

11. Sew the remaining 29-1/2" length of webbing on the lining side of purse for inside band in the same manner as in Step 9.

12. Sew buttons in place on purse front through outside band and strap with pearl cotton, referring to photo on page 68 for placement. Mark position of snap on inside band and attach snap to it following manufacturer's instructions. Edge-stitch the top edges of outside and inside bands together.

13. Use a pencil to lightly write "punkin" near the center of the off-white fabric square, referring to page 71 as a guide. Backstitch the letters with pearl cotton.

14. Trim the embroidered fabric into a 3-1/4" x 1-3/4" rectangle with the word centered. Press under a scant 1/4" on all edges of rectangle. Fuse the 2-3/4" x 1-1/4" interfacing rectangle on the back of embroidery to secure edges. Center embroidery on center front of purse 1" below webbing band. Edge-stitch in place through all layers.

Punkin Purse Center

Enlarge 150%

Cut 2 Fabric A,
2 Fabric D, and 2 interfacing

Punkin Purse
Embroidery Template

punkin

Punkin Purse side

Enlarge 150%

Cut 2 & 2 reversed Fabric B,
2 & 2 reversed Fabric C, and
2 & 2 reversed interfacing

Punkin Apron

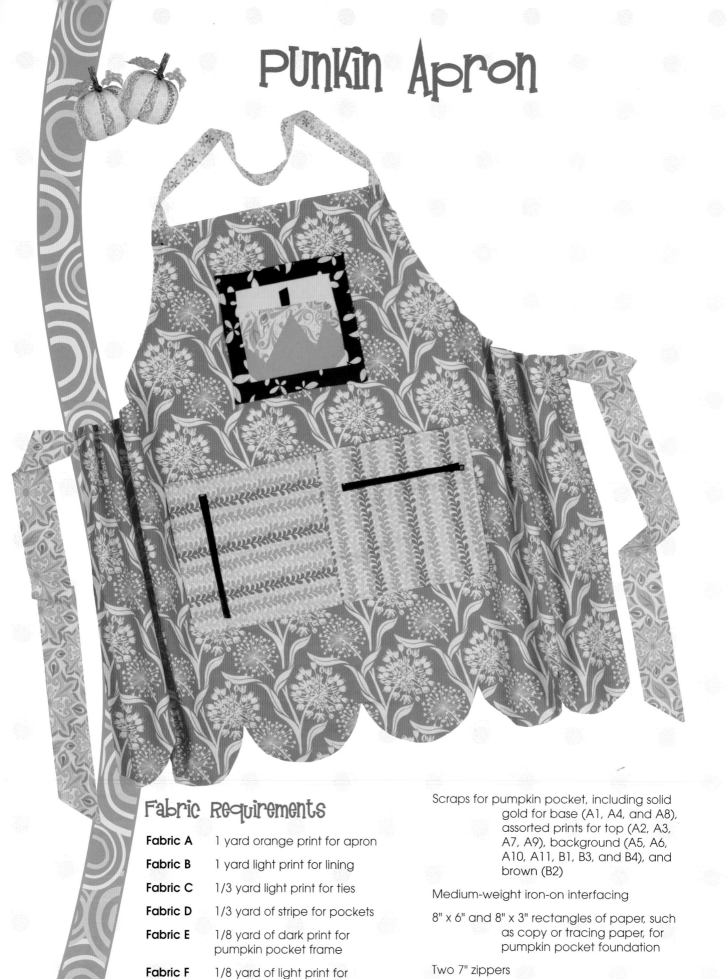

Fabric Requirements

Fabric A	1 yard orange print for apron
Fabric B	1 yard light print for lining
Fabric C	1/3 yard light print for ties
Fabric D	1/3 yard of stripe for pockets
Fabric E	1/8 yard of dark print for pumpkin pocket frame
Fabric F	1/8 yard of light print for neck strap

Scraps for pumpkin pocket, including solid gold for base (A1, A4, and A8), assorted prints for top (A2, A3, A7, A9), background (A5, A6, A10, A11, B1, B3, and B4), and brown (B2)

Medium-weight iron-on interfacing

8" x 6" and 8" x 3" rectangles of paper, such as copy or tracing paper, for pumpkin pocket foundation

Two 7" zippers

Cutting Guide

Fabric A:
- Cut 1 apron using template on page 77

Fabric B:
- Cut 1 lining using template on page 77

Fabric C:
- Cut 2 strips 5" x 30" for ties

Fabric D:
- Cut 1 rectangle 17-1/2" x 9" for lining
- Cut 2 rectangles 9" x 6-1/2" for pocket bottom
- Cut 2 rectangles 9" x 2-1/2" for pocket top
- Cut 4 rectangles 1-1/4" x 1" for pocket center

Fabric E:
- Cut 1 strip 1-1/2" x WOF for pocket frame

Fabric F:
- Cut 1 strip 3" x 23" for Small, 3" x 24" for Medium, 3" x 25" for Large and 3" x 26" for X-Large

Iron-on Interfacing:
- Cut 2 rectangles 9" x 6-1/2" for pocket bottom
- Cut 2 rectangles 9" x 2-1/2" for pocket top

Pumpkin Pocket

1. Center and trace the pumpkin and stem foundation patterns from page 76 onto your choice of foundation paper, adding a generous 1/4" seam allowance to all four sides of each pattern. The block pieces must be attached in the numerical order indicated on the patterns. Refer to the photograph on page 72 for fabric suggestions.

NOTE: *The side of the paper with the pattern lines and numbers is the BACK side of the fabric block. The blank side of the paper is the FRONT of the fabric block.*

Set machine stitching close. Smaller stitches will help perforate the paper making it easier to remove when finished.

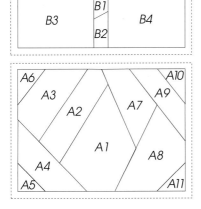

2. Cut a piece of solid gold fabric large enough to generously cover patch A1 with more than 1/4" all around. Turn the paper pattern over to the blank side. Place the A1 fabric right side facing up on the blank paper side. Hold the paper up to the light to check that the fabric covers patch A1 with more than 1/4" all around. Baste the fabric to paper by sewing through center of fabric.

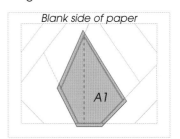

Blank side of paper

3. Cut a piece of fabric large enough to generously cover patch A2 with more than 1/4" extending around all sides. Place the fabric for patch A2 right side down on top of the A1 fabric. The two pieces will have right sides together. Pin in place.

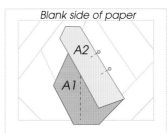

Blank side of paper

4. Turn the paper over to the printed side. Stitch on the line between patch A1 and A2, sewing carefully over pins.

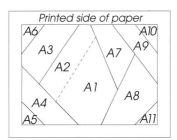

Printed side of paper

5. Turn the paper over to the blank side. Fold the paper on the just sewn seam line so traced sides will face each other and the seam allowance of A1 and A2 extends beyond fold. Use a rotary cutter to trim seam allowance to 1/4". Unfold paper and finger press A2 in place.

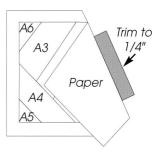

Trim to 1/4"

Paper

6. Repeat steps 3 - 5 to attach A3 - A11 pieces to foundation paper. Continue to trim each seam as in step 5 after attaching pieces. When you've added all pieces, trim the seam allowances of pumpkin section to 1/4". Remove paper.

7. Repeat paper piecing for stem section.

8. Sew together the pumpkin and stem sections with a 1/4" seam allowance to complete pumpkin center. Press seam toward stem section.

9. Measure the height of the pumpkin center. Use this measurement to cut 2 side strips from the Fabric E 1-1/2" x WOF strip. Sew these to the sides of the pumpkin center. Press seams toward strips.

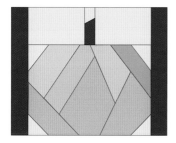

10. Measure the width of the pumpkin, including the side strips. Use this measurement to cut 2 strips from the remaining Fabric E strip. Sew these to the top and bottom of the pumpkin center to complete pumpkin block. Press seams toward strips.

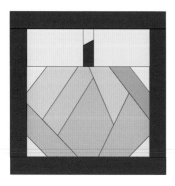

11. Use the pumpkin block as a pattern to cut a lining from any of the leftover fabrics. Sew lining to block with right sides together and a 1/4" seam allowance, leaving a 3" opening in one side edge for turning. Turn pocket right side out through opening. Press, turn under edges of opening.

Zipper Pockets

1. Fuse the appropriate iron-on interfacing rectangle to the wrong side of the Fabric D top and bottom pocket rectangles. Press under 1/4" on one 1" edge of the Fabric D 1-1/4" x 1" center rectangles as shown.

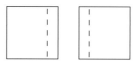

2. Using a 1/4" seam allowance, sew 2 center rectangles to the top edge of a Fabric D 9" x 6-1/2" bottom rectangle with the pressed edges toward the center. Press seam toward bottom rectangle, including the top edge of the bottom rectangle between the center rectangles.

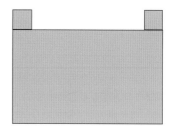

3. Sew a Fabric D 9" x 2-1/2" top rectangle to the center rectangles with a 1/4" seam allowance. Press seam toward the top rectangle, including the bottom edge of the top rectangle between the center rectangles.

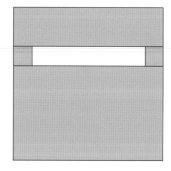

4. Center a zipper in the opening created by the rectangles. Sew the zipper in place close to the edges of the rectangles.

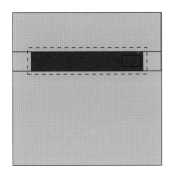

5. Repeat Steps 1-4 to make second zipper pocket.

6. Sew together the zipper pockets for pocket front as shown. Press seams toward left pocket.

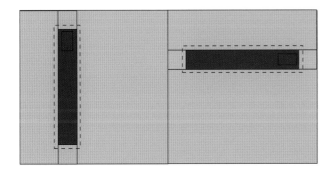

7. Sew Fabric D 17-1/2" x 9" lining to pocket front with a 1/4" seam allowance, rounding the seam at the bottom corners and leaving a 3" opening in the bottom edge for turning. Turn pocket right side out through opening. Press, turn under edges of opening.

Assembly

1. Center pumpkin pocket on apron 4" below the top edge. Sew along the side and bottom edges.

2. Center zipper pockets on apron 3-1/2" below pumpkin pocket. Sew along the side and bottom edges and down the center, dividing it in two.

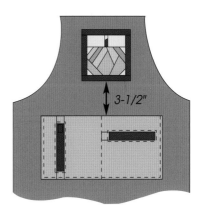

3-1/2"

3. Fold one Fabric C 5" x 30" strip in half lengthwise RST. Use a 1/4" seam allowance to sew along the long edge and then stitch across one end at an angle as shown. Trim to 1/4" seam allowance at end. Turn tie right side out. Repeat for the second tie.

4. Pin ties on apron front 3/4" below the arm edges and align the raw edges with the side edges of apron front. Sew ties in place.

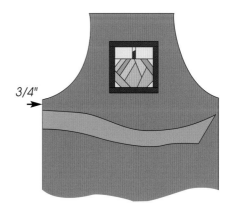

3/4"

5. Press under 1/2" on both long edges of the Fabric F neck strap. Fold the strap in half lengthwise. Sew a scant 1/8" from the long edges of the strap.

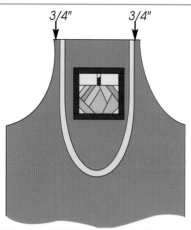

6. Pin neck strap on apron front 3/4" from the side arm edges and align the raw edges at the top. Sew strap to the apron front.

7. Sew lining to front with a 5/8" seam allowance, leaving a 6" opening in one side edge for turning. Clip seam allowances. Turn apron right side out through opening. Press, turn under edges of opening. Sew opening shut.

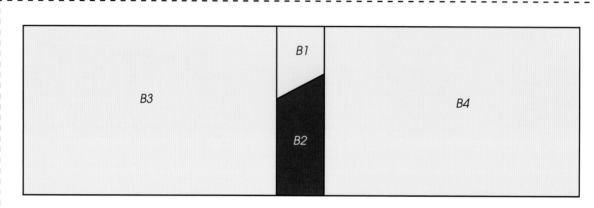

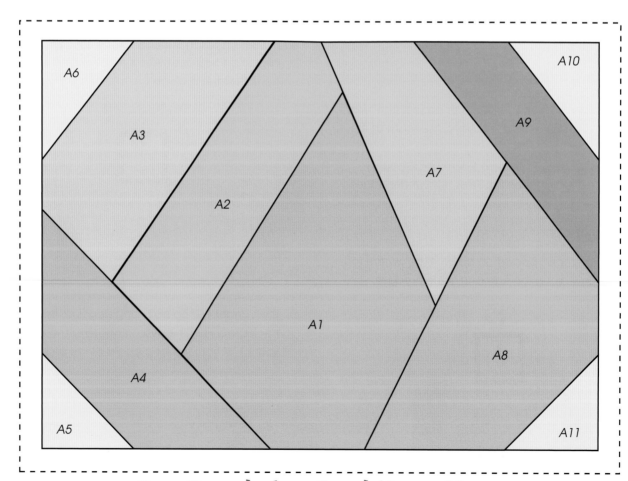

Pumpkin and stem Foundation Patterns

Neck strap

Cut 1
Small 23" x 3"
Medium 24" x 3"
Large 25" x 3"
XLarge 26" x 3"

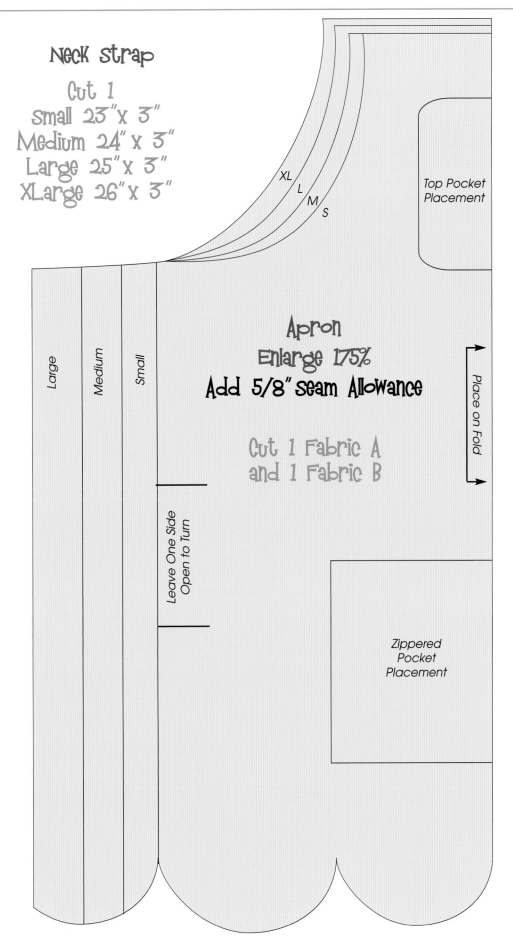

XL
L
M
S

Top Pocket
Placement

Large

Medium

Small

Apron
Enlarge 175%
Add 5/8" Seam Allowance

Cut 1 Fabric A
and 1 Fabric B

Place on Fold

Leave One Side
Open to Turn

Zippered
Pocket
Placement

Punkins

Finished sizes: approximately 5" x 11", 5" x 4" and 6-1/2" x 5-1/2"

Fabric Requirements

Small and Large Punkins
    6 assorted orange print rectangles
    9" x 13"

Medium Punkin
    11" x 20" rectangle of print fabric

Leaves   8" x 12" rectangle each of
    2 assorted green prints

Creative Grids® Curved Slotted Ruler

Short grain rice or pellets

Quart-size zip-lock bags

Steam-A-Seam 2™ Double Stick

12"-15" lengths of green wire

5" lengths of 5/8"-diameter branch for stems

Polyester fiberfill

12wt thread

Curved Rail Blocks

1. Layer 6 assorted orange print rectangles and use the ruler to cut each rectangle into 7 curved strips, following the manufacturer's instructions.

2. Sew 7 strips together as instructed and trim into an 8-1/2" x 8-1/2" curved rail block. Make 6 blocks.

Assembly

1. Sew together 2 curved rail blocks for the small punkin and 4 blocks for the large as shown, noting the direction of the strips.

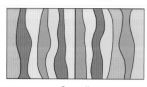

Small

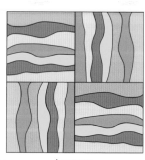

Large

2. Sew together the side edges of each punkin to form a tube; 8-1/2" edges for small, 11" edges for medium, and 16-1/2" edges for large. Press under 1/4" at the top and bottom edges of the tube.

3. Hand sew a line of basting stitches along the bottom edge of the tube and pull tightly to close; knot. Pour rice or pellets into a bag, using enough to provide a weighted base for the punkin. Place bag inside the tube and stuff the punkin with fiberfill.

4. Fold green print rectangles in half with wrong sides together to make 6" x 8" rectangles. To stiffen fabric, insert a 6" x 8" rectangle of Steam-A-Seam 2 between the fabric layers and fuse. Trace the leaf templates onto one side of the stiffened fabrics and cut out inside traced lines. Make one A and B leaf for small punkin, one A and C leaf for large punkin, and one of each leaf for medium punkin.

5. Fold a leaf in half over one end of wire. Use a zipper foot to stitch through both layers of the leaf close to the wire. Repeat for each leaf. Bend the wire into desired shape, wrapping it around a pencil to create a tendril.

6. Using a 12 wt thread, hand sew a line of basting stitches along the top edge of the tube. Place a stem in the center of the opening and stuff around it with fiberfill. Pull the basting thread, drawing the tube loosely around stem. Insert leaf tendrils in the opening, bending them into desired shape. Glue them and the stem in place. Pull basting thread to tighten top of tube around stem and tendrils; knot to secure.

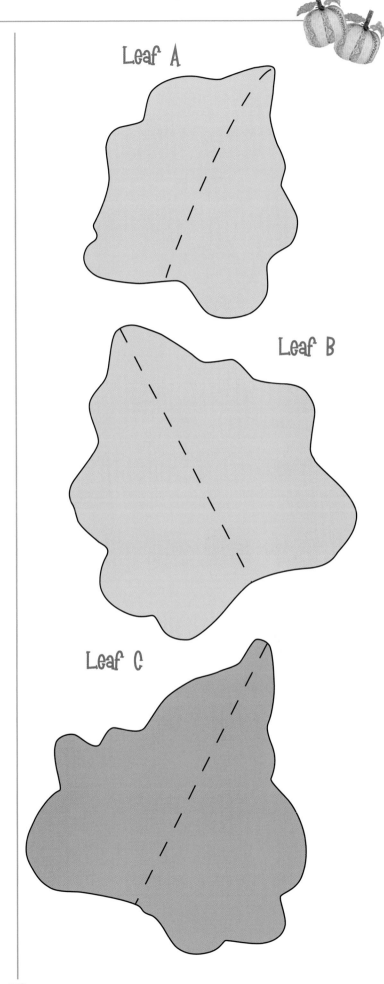

Leaf A

Leaf B

Leaf C

Credits

A special thank you to my friends at Andover Fabrics, Michael Miller Fabrics, & Robert Kaufman Fabrics who have provided many of the fabric lines used in this book. Your generosity is an invaluable resource to me and is so appreciated.